CW01099620

Churches Going Global

Connect! 2

Churches Going Global

Connect! 2

By Tim Jeffery and Ros Johnson

LIFESTYLE

SPRING HARVEST
Equipping the Church for action

Copyright © 2003 Tim Jeffery and Ros Johnson

First published in 2003 by Spring Harvest Publishing Division
and Authentic Lifestyle

09 08 07 06 05 04 03   7 6 5 4 3 2 1
Authentic Lifestyle is an imprint of Authentic Media
PO Box 300, Carlisle, Cumbria CA3 0QS, UK
and PO Box 1047, Waynesboro, GA 30830-2047, USA
www.paternoster-publishing.com

The right of Tim Jeffery and Ros Johnson to be identified as the
Authors of this Work has been asserted by them in accordance with
the Copyright, Designs and Patents Act 1988

All rights reserved. No part of this publication may be reproduced,
stored in a retrieval system, or transmitted by any means, electronic,
mechanical, photocopying, recording or otherwise, without the prior
permission of the publisher or a licence permitting restricted copying.
In the UK such licences are issued by the Copyright Licensing Agency,
90 Tottenham Court Road, London W1P 9HE

British Library Cataloguing in Publication Data

A catalogue record for this book is available from
the British Library

ISBN 1–85078–532–5

Cover design by Diane Bainbridge
Typeset by Temple Design
Printed in Great Britain by Cox & Wyman Ltd, Reading

Contents

Foreword by Steve Chalke / vii

Acknowledgements / ix

Introduction / xi

Mission / xv

1. City Gate Church, Brighton / 1
2. Glebe Farm Baptist Church
   and the Cole Valley Cluster / 11
3. Bournemouth Family Church / 23
4. The Lyndhurst Deanery / 36
5. Mexborough Wesleyan
   Reform Church, Yorkshire / 49
6. St John's, Blackheath / 57
7. Altrincham Baptist Church, Manchester / 67
8. Rugeley Community Church / 80
9. Emmanuel Church, South Croydon / 87
10. Oldmachar Church, Aberdeen / 95
11. Christ Church, Fulwood (Sheffield) / 105
12. St Saviour's, Guildford / 115
13. Basingstoke Community Churches / 121
14. Henley Baptist Church and the Equip Trust / 131

Afterword / 142

Notes on the agencies behind the Connect! Initiative / 147

Foreword

by Steve Chalke

In Matthew 22 Jesus provides us with what has to be the foundational statement for the Christian life. One that makes the rest of the Bible seem like a commentary upon it: 'Love the Lord your God with all your heart and with all your soul and with all your mind . . . Love your neighbour as yourself.' Authentic Christian faith requires both an intimacy with God and involvement in his world – one without the other leaves us incomplete and unfulfilled.

Through Faithworks, Oasis and its partners have been seeking to inspire and equip churches in the UK to get involved in their local communities and to see this as a central part of their corporate and individual life. In this globalised world however, involvement in our community has to go way beyond the people who live down the street or work in the same office. 'God so loved *the world*' and so if our involvement in and love for that world stops at the end of our street and doesn't encompass the ends of the earth – it is not very God-like.

This book of stories is an amazing testimony to the way in which ordinary people from all sorts of churches across the UK have got involved in their global community. It is not some impossible dream – even small churches can contribute to and learn from the global church – and this book proves it. I pray that in reading Churches Going Global you will be inspired at what others have done and emboldened to 'go global' too.

Acknowledgements

This book was made possible by the generosity of leaders of the churches it describes, who were willing to give up their time to tell us their stories, answer our queries, and check 'their' chapters for accuracy. We owe them our warmest thanks. The stories are all true. Inadvertently, we may have got some of the details wrong, but our intention has simply been to tell the story of what these 14 churches have been doing.

Our thanks to our partners, Hannah and Nicholas, for their faithful support and love. Also to all at Oasis who have done so much to encourage and inspire us and enrich our lives in so many ways.

Tim Jeffery, Ros Johnson
London, April 2003

Introduction

Change is in the air! Just about everywhere you look, things are changing. It sometimes feels like we are on a runaway train with changes coming thicker and faster all the time. In the Christian community we are grappling anew with what church is all about and how it's going to look in the future. Our understanding of the message of the gospel and how we communicate it into a predominantly post-modern context is a growing discussion that is likely to develop much further. In these shifting sands, it was always unlikely that our understanding and practice of global mission would remain unaffected. In fact, in the early twenty-first century, we are in the middle of a paradigm shift in global mission. The whole way we conceive of and do global mission is not just getting a facelift but is undergoing fundamental change. The Connect! Initiative is seeking to explore and attempt to articulate some of these changes and to help the church take hold of the opportunities of an exciting new era.

The first book in the Connect series[1] came at the issue of Christians' involvement in the world from a theoretical base. It argued that because of fundamental changes happening in the world, there are new opportunities for all Christian people to take up Christ's call to be involved in Judea, Samaria and to the ends of the earth. In a globalised era, one no longer has to don a pith helmet and set sail for decades of missionary service to be involved in global mission. Each one of us already has an impact on the rest of the world through the things we buy and the way we live. As Christians, we have a calling and

---

[1] *Connect!* by Tim Jeffrey with Steve Chalke, published in 2003 by Authentic.

responsibility to be involved in what God is doing in different parts of the world – as well as being involved in our own local neighbourhood.

Theory is fine and can help to place a framework on complex issues. However, much of the time people don't seem to need to be convinced of the 'why'. It would seem for instance that, for many people, it is self-evident that Christians should be involved in the world. The barrier to actually doing something is not doubt over whether it is right (the 'why'), but an imagination gap – the 'how' or the 'what'. So rather than make another book of slightly disembodied suggestions, we felt it would be better simply to fire people's imaginations with stories of what groups of Christians across the UK are already doing.

One of the characteristics of paradigm shifts in any field is that people will make the change at different speeds. Some will be scared at the thought of losing the security of the traditional ways that seem to have served well in the past. Others will be the early-adopters who, sometimes unwittingly, will step in to the new territory and begin exploring well before the terrain has been mapped out and new roads built into it. This book gives examples of some of these early-adopters. Their stories are very different – some have really just gone a few steps into the new world but others have struck out far into uncharted territory.

One of the highlights in the process of developing Connect! has been getting to know churches already getting directly stuck in to global mission. It has been refreshing and exciting to find more and more such churches. The stories of what they are doing globally and the impact on them and their mission locally are captivating, and graphically illustrate the realities of this emerging era of global mission. Indeed, what better way to understand a new era than to hear stories from those who are already pioneering pathways into the future? This book is therefore a book of stories, illustrating from real examples the joys and sorrows, lessons and pitfalls that are beginning to emerge.

In mission circles something of a myth seems to have grown that churches are likely to mess it up if they get directly involved in mission without the help of a mission agency. What we found as we researched were churches large and small that had – often for several years – been actively and directly involved in a whole range of mission activities. What's more, they were doing it well and being transformed in the process.

The churches featured in this book vary widely in almost every way and also in the types of mission activities they are undertaking. The stories themselves are very different too, but it is fascinating to see that they all have one thing in common. They all demonstrate that 'mission direct' only works if it is founded on sound, trusting relationships between the individuals who are actively involved in building and maintaining the link. In fact that is the main message of this book: relationship is the basis from which everything has to start.

Another common feature of these stories is that in almost every instance at least one person said to us: 'You know, we have gained far more than we have given.' The church link may have started out of a desire by a British church to help a church in a poorer country, but the impact of a personal encounter with materially poor but spiritually rich Christians in another culture has often been a life-changing experience for the British Christians. We have so much to learn from our Christian brothers and sisters on other continents, if only our eyes, ears and hearts can be open to receive. In fact, it seems true to say that in getting involved with the global church, churches in the UK are finding a growing depth and renewal in their own faith.

If you are seeking renewal in your own church, it may just be that you will find part of the way forward somewhere else within the global church. Read these stories, see how it has worked for other people, and consider what God may be saying to you and your church about your involvement to the ends of the earth.

If your church is contemplating starting a link with a church in another country or is in the early stages of getting one started, these stories contain a fund of practical experience and advice. To help you pick out stories that illustrate particular points, we have included a guide to the chapters by topic and country. But if you are just reading out of general interest, our hope is that you will be intrigued, amazed and encouraged to learn how God can use people like you in his global mission.

Mission, whether round the corner or halfway across the world, should be the heartbeat of the church. We hope that the stories in this book show that it is possible – even desirable – for global mission to be central to the life of every church.

Tim Jeffery and Ros Johnson
Oasis Trust, London
May 2003

Mission

I could tell of the young man bathing the AIDS patient.
Of teenagers moved to tears by the plight of the poor.
And left speechless by the eloquence of their dance.
I have heard the singing of an African church
And the praying of an Indian one.
I have been given everything
From a family who have nothing.
I have seen rich westerners
Sharing their lives with the poor
And coming home richer.
I have seen the problems of some disappear
As they touch the needy.
And I have seen the joy of developing partnership.
I have seen that mission is not optional,
I have seen it is the heart, the voice and the dance of God.

by Dave Day

Dave is a team leader at Bristol Christian Fellowship and part of the Pioneer International Coordinators Team. He works extensively with churches in India, Africa, Europe and the USA.

1

City Gate Church, Brighton

> **GLOBAL LINKS:** *South Africa and Cambodia*
>
> **CONGREGATION SIZE (2003):** *around 150*
>
> **CHURCH GROUPING:** *Independent, a member of the Pioneer Church Network*

City Gate Church (CGC) originated as a group of friends meeting regularly to eat, talk and pray in the late seventies. Andy Au was one of this first group and has been involved ever since. He remembers back to those early days: 'As the friendships deepened we felt God started to speak to us and add to our number so that by 1982 we were a community of 50 people who then attended different churches. That year, we felt that God was calling us to establish a church because we found it hard to find in any local church the depth and reality of relationship which we were experiencing together. We asked the members of the group to decide where their 'home' was – in their current churches or in the group. Most decided to stay in their current churches, and only 12 were left to form the City Gate Church. Our vision right from the start was to be a community within the community, reaching out to that community.' At this stage Andy gave up his secular job to work for the church where he is still the senior pastor.

From 1982-92 their numbers grew slowly to about thirty, and until about 1998 all their members lived very locally. In that period of slow growth and consolidation Andy recognises that 'our DNA was formed.' He believes God was and is preparing CGC for what church is to become in a post-modern age. Their strap-line drawn up in that period reads: 'Together for God, each other and the nations.' They were consciously trying to do church in a way that was strongly relational and real. They learnt how to be a family. This meant not glossing over differences, but facing up to them and talking them through. The concept of having a 'covenant relationship' with each other is very important. Andy defines the core of 'covenant' as 'I will never leave you or forsake you' – a deep level of commitment, as if the others were members of your own family. They also developed a relational, organic, church structure.

In early 2003 the 150-strong membership of CGC (now part of the Pioneer church network) was a reasonable cross-section of local people. There are many teachers and artists, some nurses, but few other 'professionals' in the congregation – it is not a rich church. Its total income in 2002 was about £138,000, of which 18.5 per cent went on overseas mission.

Mission to the local community and internationally

CGC is based out of a multi-purpose centre which is designed to serve their community as well as accommodate church activities. It is used by a range of secular groups with about 500-800 non-churchgoing local residents now using the building each week. One of the services offered is the provision of 6,000 meals per week for the homeless and other needy people in Brighton, to which CGC is a major contributor. This service costs £100,000 a year, of which up to 30 per cent comes from a grant, with fundraising and donations providing the rest.

Andy comments, 'The church is strongly outward-looking. 90 per cent of our members are mobilised for mission in the UK and beyond, and of the eight leaders, five are focused outside CGC. Little of the mission work that we have become involved in is the result of plans and strategies. We tend to try to follow where we feel God is leading.'

Links with South Africa

In 1991 Andy and others at CGC hosted some overseas visitors attending a World Charismatic Leaders' Meeting in Brighton. One of their guests was Dr Joseph Kobo, founder and leader of an indigenous church movement – Anointed Voice of Africa – in the Eastern Cape, South Africa. There are currently about two hundred and fifty churches in this group, with congregations ranging in size from 25 to 1,000. The two men struck up a strong friendship, and visits were exchanged in both directions over the next few years.

One of the early highlights occurred in 1994 when two members of one of Joseph Kobo's churches spent a couple of months in Brighton with the people of CGC. Both of these men came from poor communities – one had never seen a plane or even been out of the Eastern Cape. They came partly to learn, but they spent much of their time praying for CGC, sharing and encouraging church members. They told many stories of revival and miracles from their own experience of God working in their communities. 'They gave far more than they received from us,' said Andy.

From the start Dr Kobo was keen to link up with a church grouping in the UK but for several years this did not happen. In 1999 he asked Andy if he could link with Pioneer. Andy warned him that Pioneer did not have money to give away, and that they would want to satisfy themselves over some practices in Joseph's church. He replied that money was not his prime interest; first and foremost he wanted help in running his churches and wanted to be accountable to someone – preferably in the UK. Although Andy was not a senior leader in the Pioneer movement, he wanted Andy to be that person as he felt that Andy understood both him and his people and that there was a strong relationship between them.

Andy felt that if this relationship were to work, he would need to get to know Joseph's church network much better. Since that time CGC has been sending teams to the Eastern Cape to build on this relationship and have focused on two villages in particular. They feel they need to get inside the network and build 'family' style relationships, just as they have from the earliest days of CGC.

In September 2002 Andrea Mason, an elder from CGC, and her husband Andy went out and built a mud hut in Mampondomiseni, one of the two villages to which they are particularly closely connected. Andrea says: 'This was a practical demonstration of our affirmation that they are our family, and a declaration that we're there for the long haul and investing our lives and families with theirs. The hut is a physical presence, like a seed, to remind them that we're thinking of them and praying for them. We brought some things back from the village, like a clay head made by one of the villagers, which we keep in our house in Brighton. We told them that we've brought something of them back with us, as a physical reminder of them and what they mean to us. It is all part of building relationship person to person, family to family, church to church.'

CGC contributed to the cost of a new church building in Mampondomiseni, and five members of CGC were invited to the opening ceremony in September 2000. While they were there, they attended a memorial service which the church was organising for the whole community, in memory of warriors from the village who had died in the English Channel in the First World War. It was only during this service attended by about a thousand people that Andy and the others from CGC heard the tragic story of what had happened 83 years earlier.

Healing after 83 years

In response to a plea from Britain for help with the war effort, Chief Henry Bokleni Ndamase of Mampondomiseni called together his warriors to travel to England as part of the South African Native Labour Corps. They were to become trench diggers and stretcher bearers. They went first to England and then set out for France from Plymouth in February 1917 on the troopship SS Mendi. They never reached France because the Mendi was rammed in thick fog by another allied ship, and sank in the English Channel off St Catherine's Point, Isle of Wight. It was said that the South Africans, led by their own chaplain, sang and performed a traditional death dance on the deck as the ship sank within twenty minutes. Although the other ship lingered at the site of the collision for several hours, it only lowered one lifeboat to pick up survivors, an action later described by a court as inexcusable.

Tragically, 647 black South Africans were lost. Their home communities were devastated. To make matters worse, the tragedy was largely covered up by the British Government to avoid lowering morale, and rural families received little information about what had happened, still less an apology. The story has been largely ignored by historians until recent years. Those who died are commemorated on memorials in Southampton, France, Soweto and at a town near Pretoria, but the relatives of the rural dead from Transkei in the Eastern Cape were not informed or involved in the establishment of these memorials.

The CGC team realised during the memorial service that despite the lapse in time since these events, there was still a very real grief that the community had not been able to work through. The British group felt they needed to respond to the feelings being expressed. Andy recalls the moment: 'After consulting with the others in our group, I knelt down on the platform and, on behalf of the British people, thanked the community for their generous response in the UK's hour of need. I apologised for the apparent indifference of the British Government, and asked for their forgiveness.'

This simple act temporarily flummoxed the community, which included Chief Malizole, a grandson of Chief Henry who had drowned. After some discussion, there was a deeply moving response of spoken forgiveness from the elders and community. One of the CGC members who were there wrote later: 'Chief Malizole and each of the elders embraced their guests with a determination and strength, which spoke far louder than words ever could. Their graciousness, willingness to forgive and unfathomable generosity were truly humbling, yet totally releasing. The tears and pain of repentance were absorbed into those powerful hugs of acceptance and love. It was a forgiveness that can only be given by those who have known the forgiveness, acceptance and unconditional love of Christ themselves. Together we had touched the healing of Christ's ministry of reconciliation.'

That was not the end however. The visitors from CGC felt that they had to ensure that a memorial was set up in England with a ceremony involving the relatives and community of those who had died. The place they chose was Newtimber churchyard, in West Sussex, on the family estate of Earl Sydney Buxton who was Governor-General of South Africa in 1917 and had a great love for the people. The ceremony took place in June 2002 and thirty people attended from the Nyandeni district. The South African Foreign Minister, High Commissioner and Deputy High Commissioner also came. In September 2002 a team of twenty-five from CGC and other Pioneer churches went back to South Africa to 'turn the sod' for another memorial being set up in Nyandeni district.

Because of this spontaneous initiative by CGC they were asked by the South African Government to act as a channel to encourage UK interest and involvement in Transkei and its development, notably in the areas of health, education and business. A memorandum of understanding was signed between that Government and CGC for this purpose. Visits in each direction intensified. Dr Kobo and his church network were keen to be involved as major change agents in their communities, and Andy also made contacts with municipality and traditional leaders in South Africa, and with politicians, local councils and churches in the UK. It is hoped that involvement will be broadened out beyond Christian organisations, but that those who get involved will have similar relational values.

One idea is to 'twin' churches in the UK with 'zones' of the church network in Transkei, in the belief that real friendships that go deep into people's lives are more sustainable than projects. 'Rank and file' church members are being encouraged to make connections – not just church leaders. There is no long-term plan other than to develop long lasting relationships in South Africa. 'Who knows what will happen! It was all an accident!' says Andy. 'But it all came from taking to South Africa the lessons we at City Gate have learnt from practising reconciliation in our own community.'

Cambodia

Back in the 1980s, Andy Au went on a visit to Cambodia and Thailand. Following this visit, CGC successfully established a fish farm in Thailand, which was then handed over to a local evangelist to provide him with income.

In the early nineties Andy joined the board of Southeast Asian Outreach, a small mission agency focused solely on Cambodia, which had until then seen its role as primarily to pray for that devastated country. With Andy's encouragement however, it decided to set up some development projects with the aim of being 'good news' to the land. A project called SCALE was established in 1991 by agreement with the Cambodian Government, to help farmers establish fish farms and to give them support and training to improve their farming of fruit and vegetables. Farmer-led research projects were also conducted. Andy's brother spent several years in Cambodia helping to run the project. Thousands of farmers have now been helped, and in 2003 the project was being handed over to local ownership. Those who came to serve on the project (from CGC and other Pioneer churches) also witnessed to their Christian faith, and a church was established at one of the SCALE development centres.

Andy comments: 'Factionalism was a serious problem in Cambodia, and relationships frequently broke down. It affected the local church, most agencies working there, and visiting Christians. This was due in part to the spiritual climate in the country and also to the fact that members of visiting multi-national teams were not covenanted to each other and attended many different churches in Cambodia. The net result was that whilst teams of professionals were doing useful developmental work, they were having limited impact spiritually. I have come to believe that building strong covenant relationships has to be a priority, with practical projects springing from these.'

Andrea Mason describes how CGC believe that God has confirmed to them their involvement in Cambodia: 'A young Christian woman of Cambodian Chinese origin living in the United States had been brought up feeling ashamed and confused about her Cambodian background. In 1994 she was told by God to "go to England for your healing and to discover your roots". Shortly after arriving in Brighton she came to a Sunday morning service at CGC. The first thing she noticed was a Cambodian scarf. Then she heard a report on a trip to Cambodia from which a number of us had just returned. This seemed more than a coincidence! She became a member of CGC until her return to the States. As a result of her stay with us she was able to get a full picture of her Cambodian history. She started praying for that nation, resolved the personal confusion that she had felt, and was able to accept her own identity as a Cambodian Chinese.'

Something similar happened almost exactly a year later when a young British man who had become a Christian in Cambodia visited City Gate Church on his return to the UK. Again on his first visit he saw Cambodian scarves, and heard people talking about a trip there from which they had recently returned. Church leaders felt clearly that God must be in what was happening, confirming their involvement in Cambodia. CGC is itself planning to build a church in Cambodia. In keeping with their experience of and belief in relationships, they will first visit regularly, pray with people there and build strong, covenant relationships.

CGC's attitude to global mission

For CGC, mission is the outworking in relationship of God's love for the world. 'UK Christians can contribute money and expertise to the wider church,' Andy says, 'but the best thing we can give is relationships. We have to go in humility and vulnerability, and be ready to receive. Reconciliation at all levels is central.'

If you would like to discuss twinning your church with a 'zone' in South Africa, contact:

Andy Au
City Gate Church
84-86 London Road
Brighton BN1 4JF
Tel: 0273 693870
Email: karen@citygatechurch.org.uk

2

Glebe Farm Baptist Church
and The Cole Valley Cluster

GLOBAL LINKS: *Brazil and South Korea*

CONGREGATION SIZE (2003): *about 20 adults (Glebe Farm Baptist only)*

DENOMINATION: *Baptist*

'A pastor's graveyard' was the description of East Birmingham given to one church leader who was moving there. Indeed parts of this disadvantaged area of the city can be very difficult and dispiriting for both 'ordinary' Christians and church leaders. Unemployment is high and aspirations are low. Drugs, crime and vandalism seem to lurk around every corner.

Birmingham has a long tradition of individualism and entrepreneurialism which, while beneficial to the economic development of the area in the past, has often had a negative impact on church unity. Cooperation between churches has not been a strong feature of the Christian community – on a visit to the city Billy Graham observed that 'Birmingham is a hotbed of interdenominational strife.'

Against this backdrop, the pastors of a group of Baptist churches in East Birmingham started, in the early nineties, to meet regularly together for fellowship and mutual support. Close and trusting relationships were built up between the ministers and in 1998, when three of the ministers were moving on, it was decided to open the group up to other leaders and church members. Deacons and leadership teams started meeting together. Churches began undertaking joint events and services that involved much wider groups from within the congregations. The depth of relationship that had developed amongst the pastors began to spread across the church membership. This group of churches became known as the 'Cole Valley Cluster' and has grown to seven member churches of various denominations. All the churches are small with the largest having only 100 members.

Glebe Farm Baptist Church (GFB), with about twenty adult members, is one of the smallest churches in the cluster and has two part-time pastors, John Cate and John Alvis. Newbridge Baptist, also in the cluster, is led by Frank Sherburn and has around fifty members.

The link with Brazil

In the mid nineties David Brennand, then pastor of Glebe Farm Baptist, made contact through a neighbouring church in West Bromwich with some Brazilians who were visiting Birmingham. They were members of a Brazilian mission group called Transcultural Mission and included a pastor called Valmir from a large church in the Brazilian city of Joinville. Through that group he met members of Go to the Nations (GTTN), another Brazilian mission group that a few years earlier had begun to send members to build links with churches in Britain. He felt immediately that there was something special about them: 'They had an anointing.' In 1996 he visited Marcos Barros and other members of GTTN who were then based in Edinburgh, and a few months later a group of Brazilians came to Glebe Farm and encouraged members of the church to attend a GTTN conference in the city of Uberlandia, Brazil.

David decided to go to this conference and there he met up again with Valmir. During the trip he developed serious trouble with a detached retina in one of his eyes and ended up spending some time in Joinville with Valmir and members of his church. A friendship developed between the two pastors, and David was deeply moved by the warmth of the Brazilian hospitality. At that time the Joinville church had a problem with one of its leaders, and was uncertain how to handle it. But David had had experience of very similar problems in England and was able to give them helpful and timely advice. This encouraged him to see that there was real potential for this relationship to be mutual and creative, despite the huge disparity in numbers between the two churches.

Six months later two other members of Glebe Farm, John Alvis and Martin Crawford, visited the church in Joinville. Over the next few years the relationship between the churches was strengthened by regular visits by people from the two congregations which began to spread amongst a number of churches in the Cole Valley Cluster.

What is Go to the Nations?

In the early 1990s a network of church leaders with a passion for evangelism came together in areas of Brazil which had been deeply touched by ongoing revival. They felt God was challenging them to get involved in world mission and to do so through partnership and shared resources. Their original vision was to reach some of the least evangelised countries, but God drew them to establish a European base in the UK. Inspired by Malachi 4:6a they believed God was calling them back to their 'spiritual fathers' in the UK, through whom the gospel had first reached Brazil. They also believed that, by combining Brazilian enthusiasm with British maturity and experience in mission, they could build a partnership in mission that would be more effective than either nationality acting in isolation. Go to the Nations is now a network of Brazilian and European churches of different denominations and backgrounds.

The first Brazilian missionaries to the UK – including Marcos Barros and his family – arrived in 1993 and found churches around the country willing to receive them to work in joint ministry within the local church and community. While Marcos and his family have remained in the UK to encourage the work, other Brazilians have come and gone, often spending a year or two joining in the life of a local church. The Brazilians aim to infect UK churches with their passion for relationships, prayer and worship. Visits to Brazil are also arranged so that British Christians can experience the strong community, enthusiasm and love which are such a big part of church life there. The contacts have had a transforming effect on many of those involved.

Some of the Brazilians who came to the UK have moved on to third countries, usually with financial and prayer support from their UK church as well as their home church in Brazil. GTTN sees the whole mission-building process as long-term.

This slow building of the relationship took a dramatic turn in 1999 when 17 young people from Joinville came to East Birmingham for three weeks. Although some activities such as English classes, sightseeing and prayer walking were planned for the trip, the main aim was simply 'to get to know you' and share lives. For many at the receiving end in Birmingham this visit brought home some of the very distinct cultural differences between the two churches. When one of the Brazilian group's leaders was asked what he intended to achieve during the trip, he replied: 'I have come to be with you. My big aim is to be with you.' In their task-oriented culture the British hosts found this difficult at first, but soon came to value the Brazilian prioritisation of relationships, and the depth of trust and friendship that resulted.

This focus on relationships has been the single biggest lesson that the churches in Birmingham have learnt from their Brazilian friends. Seeing it lived out, experiencing the quality of relationship amongst the Brazilians, and being included into those relationships has had a transforming effect.

Frank Sherburn comments: 'For the Brazilians, the important thing is relationship and the sheer joy of being together. Those of us more accustomed to British reserve at first found them frighteningly open, but there was also something deeply attractive about the quality and depth of relationships. It made me realise that they had something that we needed, and I decided never to settle for second best in relationships again.'

A visit to Joinville in 2000 by John Cate and John Alvis (who by now had succeeded David Brennand as joint part-time pastors) so convinced them that 'relationships were totally important' if their church was to grow, that they decided to take positive steps to put relationships at the heart of GFB's life. 'We stopped meeting in our church building and held all services instead in John Cate's large living room. There was opposition from some quarters at first, but the move was hugely significant for dynamics within the church. As we look back now we realise that the shift we were making was to stop doing church and start being church. We saw some fantastic changes begin to occur as loving relationships grew within the congregation, and members who had previously been rather passive began to take a much more active part in church life.'

Newbridge Baptist Church is more traditional, but there too the lessons learnt from the Brazilians have been applied. 'The church leaders have encouraged members to share their personal lives with each other, which has meant being vulnerable and taking risks. Hospitality both within our congregation and with others in the cluster has been very important. It has been a great blessing. There has been a huge shift. Relationships are totally changed, and there's a real sense of family,' says Frank.

Learning about discipling

The experience of sharing their homes with the Brazilians, and spending quality time with them, enabled the British hosts to see further into the lives of their new friends. One of the amazing things they began to discover was the incredible depth of trust that existed between members of one Joinville church cell group and its group leader. They learnt that members of the group would ask the leader for guidance on very personal matters such as who to marry, or what their next job should be. If the cell group leader himself felt in need of advice he would consult with other group leaders before responding to such questions. The cell group leader, asked about his responsibilities, commented simply: 'Over a period of time, you lay down your life for your cell group.'

The British leaders were deeply impressed by the way that discipling of church members was an integral part of community life in the Joinville congregation. Frank says: 'At first I was concerned about the high level of risk of putting so much power into the hands of church leaders. We know that situations like this have led to abuse or "heavy shepherding". But being able to talk about this with the people involved, and see the wonderful levels of trust within relationships, eased those fears – we saw no evidence of such abuse.'

The church leaders also became aware that there were other spiritual dimensions to these contacts. Almost every visit to or from Brazil was accompanied by a serious illness afflicting those involved or their close relatives. But God also gave healing in such circumstances. For example, during one visit by people from Joinville, Ruth Cate, one of John's daughters, fell seriously ill and ended up in intensive care in hospital. John says: 'Ruth collapsed at home and was rushed to hospital. Her blood count was critically low and she needed a series of blood transfusions on two separate occasions to keep her alive. But prayer was answered and Ruth was restored to full health very quickly. To this day the doctors have been unable to establish the cause. Wherever God moves, the enemy attacks but He is sovereign and we can trust Him.'

The faith and spirituality of the Brazilians have often given personal encouragement to the British leaders. John Cate recalls: 'I had felt rather embarrassed at the huge difference in size between our tiny church at Glebe Farm and the far bigger congregation at Joinville. We were building a bridge between hundreds of people in Joinville and only about twenty in Glebe Farm – the imbalance was a real source of discomfort for me and felt very unequal. On one visit I shared with our Brazilian friends how I felt about this. Afterwards a Brazilian prophesied that God was saying that he was building this bridge, and it was as perfect at the British end as it was at the Brazilian. What an encouragement!

'We have also been encouraged to believe that God is demolishing strongholds in Birmingham and that over time things here will change. We believe that the first stronghold to be demolished in Cole Valley was the stronghold of the independent spirit, which had hampered cooperation between churches. There is still a long way to go with this but we have seen dramatic changes that we hope will be an inspiration to inter-church cooperation in other parts of the city.'

The cluster continues to evolve and grow together. They have begun to think of setting up a team ministry, and a Brazilian church leader is hoping to come to work with them for six to twelve months. The Brazilians are also keen to build links with the Koreans who form the other main international link for the Cole Valley Cluster.

The South Korean connection

In 1998 a young man named Chang Soo-Park was praying at home in Korea. 'I was asking God to show me more of the vision he had for my life. God reminded me that I am part of a worldwide church and that our job is worldwide mission. After exploring various options I felt God calling me to the UK and came to Birmingham in October 1999, eager to learn a lot from British Christians, whose ancestors had brought the gospel to so many parts of the world.' However Chang was shocked and disappointed at the state of the church in Britain – its low morale, loss of passion and lack of evangelistic zeal. In order to improve his English, he worked for some months in a day centre for people with learning difficulties. Then in 2001 he started an MA course in Applied Theology at Queen's College,

Birmingham, part of which involved a short-term assignment at Newbridge Baptist Church. Through this he joined the Cole Valley Cluster.

Chang soon built up good relationships with many people from different churches in the cluster, and began to pray earnestly for those churches and for the whole city. 'A desire to see revival in Birmingham touched my heart, and burnt there. I felt that God was calling me to commit myself to this place and these people.' In June 2002 he told the cluster leaders that he wanted to stay in the city and work for revival there. The leaders were deeply touched and challenged at the depth of his love and commitment when he told them: 'I want to die in this country.'

There was however the question of how he could be funded to stay in the UK. At that time he was not supported by any mission agency, and Korean mission agencies generally did not see Europe as a mission field. However the leader of the Korean All-Nations Mission (KAM) visited Chang and the cluster that summer. As a result of what the KAM leader saw of the state of the British church, he radically altered his own – and the agency's – outlook, and built a new strategy which included Europe among the regions needing Christian mission work from Korea. One of the results was that the KAM affirmed Chang's call to stay in Birmingham, and agreed to provide half the funding to enable him to do so. Newbridge Baptist Church agreed to provide the other half and appointed him as associate pastor.

In addition to his passionate commitment to serving God in Birmingham, Chang is deeply concerned to change Korean ways of doing mission and their perception that cross-cultural mission is needed only in the Third World. Chang wants the realisation that western countries are also a mission field, which the KAM has now taken on board, to be accepted more widely. The Korean church is very divided denominationally, and Chang feels deeply that Korean Christians should be more ready to cooperate with Christians of other nationalities and denominations for mission.

Chang has had to overcome considerable cultural and language differences in order to become part of church life in Cole Valley, but the cluster church leaders are in no doubt that they are learning a huge amount from him. They say: 'He is brave enough to have a vision that God gives. The Korean church is brave – their whole attitude is about faith. You don't have to work out how it can be done before taking on a vision. Their prayer life is in a different dimension. Chang is constantly challenging us on commitment, trust, and the need to live in the future, where prayer is answered. It's like the Koreans have an extra gear. When the rubber hits the road and things get hard, they just move up a gear.'

Chang is also learning and gaining through working in the cluster. He recognises that in Korea pastors are often given a very elevated position within the church and can be autocratic and somewhat remote from their congregations, but in Birmingham he has learnt a more approachable style of pastoring.

Cluster leaders have had the opportunity to share in Korea something of what they have learnt from the Brazilians. In August 2002 some of them went to Korea, where the main theme of their preaching and teaching was the significance of relationships, a message which is as relevant for Korean churches as it is for British. This link is developing and plans are in place for further visits in the coming years.

The emerging vision for Cole Valley

So what do all these international contacts mean in practical terms for the Cole Valley Cluster? The leaders say they believe they are being built into a 'safe pair of hands' that God can use, but that they are still in the early stages. The churches run some projects for the local community and have undertaken joint outreach events, but there is a rising impatience to move out beyond their own premises and groups of Christian friends to build more links with the wider community. John Cate is optimistic about the future: 'We are seeing Jesus' presence with us, especially as we build relationships and work together.'

However God may have still more ambitious plans for them. After it was confirmed that he could stay in Birmingham, Chang continued to pray for the city and to ask for a vision for the cluster. In November 2002 he shared with cluster leaders a vision that he believed God had given him over a three-day period. It is a very ambitious vision, which the cluster leaders say they could never have produced themselves, involving Koreans and Brazilians as well as the local people in East Birmingham. Covering about ten pages, it proclaims the need for Christians to work together regardless of race, nationality, culture or denomination, and presents a vision of the cluster becoming a loving community reaching out in holistic mission, and challenging other churches to do the same. It speaks of a dream of sending out 'hundreds of our members as career missionaries and church workers to every continent' – challenging targets indeed for a group of Christians then numbering only around three hundred!

It also proposes building on the growing relationships with Korean and Brazilian Christians by setting up a centre in Birmingham to provide training in English, cultural awareness and theology, to which Christians from both countries could come to be equipped for mission.

The cluster leaders were awed and excited by Chang's proposals, and after prayerful consideration they adopted it as the vision for the cluster. They started to explore the practical issues around setting up the proposed mission

training centre, and found several things coming together
to give them encouragement in an amazing way. Cluster
leaders plan that the students who come to the centre will
be integrated into the lives of cluster members and their
churches. The KAM agency also responded favourably to
the vision and is considering giving scholarships to assist
students going to train in Birmingham.

What is God saying?

Church leaders in the Cole Valley Cluster realise that it is
probably too early to discern fully what God may be
saying to them through the bringing together in
Birmingham of people and influences from such disparate
parts of the world. Part of it, they think, is about being
available for God to build bridges through them.

Frank Sherburn and John Cate are totally convinced of
the benefits of their contacts with Brazil and Korea: 'God is
teaching us to love each other so that he can release his
power. For us, the experience of those communities shown
in the Transformation videos[2] has come alive. When
pastors and churches can come together and forget their
parochialism and jealousies, God starts to work. We have
to work together. There is only one church. Our experience
of working together with Christians from other countries
is that in doing this, God blesses everyone.'

---

[2] The two *Transformations* videos tell the stories of communities
in several continents which have been transformed by the power
of God. In almost every case, things began to happen when the
churches in each community started to cooperate and seek God
together. The videos can be obtained from: Evangelical Films,
Danbury Common Old Mission, The Common, Danbury,
Chelmsford, Essex CM3 4EE. Telephone 01245 226642.

3

Bournemouth Family Church

GLOBAL LINKS: *Uganda*

CONGREGATION SIZE (2003): *around 350*

CHURCH GROUPING: *New Frontiers International*

Bournemouth Family Church (formerly called the New Covenant Church) has a deep passion for mission and an amazing commitment to it. The church was started as a church plant in 1994 by a nucleus of committed Christians from an NFI church nearby. It has about two hundred and fifty members, although the average Sunday congregation is around three hundred and fifty, and supports three full-time elders. Ken Matthews is the elder with primary responsibility for evangelism and mission. He and his wife Sue have been involved with Bournemouth Family Church from the beginning, as they joined in the church planting while they were training at nearby Moorlands Bible College, and committed themselves to the church when their course finished.

New Frontiers International

New Frontiers International (NFI) is a network of churches led by Terry Virgo that now embraces over two hundred churches on four continents. It sees its mission as to 'Advance the Kingdom of God by restoring the church, making disciples, training leaders, planting churches and reaching the nations.' With a strong emphasis on the exposition of Scripture, charismatic gifts and the power of the Holy Spirit, and a firm belief in the autonomy of the local church, the network is built and maintained by relationship and a common sense of mission. Their outward focus includes social action as well as evangelism.

The Vision Statement for Bournemouth Family Church (BFC), drawn up in 1999, provides a strong motivating force for the work they do. It reads

To spread a passion for the glory of the Son by
- Making disciples (they train leaders every year and aim to give many away to new NFI churches)
- Touching and healing (the poor and needy – including drug addicts and prostitutes in the Bournemouth area)
- Going to the Nations and reaching the 'Unreached'.

The principles underlying this vision statement guided the church plant from its early days, inspired by the passion of its leaders, the church's understanding of biblical priorities and prophetic input from itinerant but well-known apostolic teachers and leaders. The centrality of the vision statement to the life of the church is demonstrated by the fact that the statement is brought to the attention of those wanting to join the church. If they feel they cannot share this vision, they are encouraged to look at other churches in the town that might suit them better.

The church's budget is split three ways to support these three goals, although through special appeals, overseas mission can actually take up to 40 per cent of the church's income in any year.

Motivation to mission

Ken points to a number of key Bible passages that have been crucial in motivating people in BFC to mission

- Isaiah 58 – in which God tells his people to spend themselves for the poor and needy
- Matthew 25 – the parable of the sheep and the goats
- Matthew 28:16-20 – The Great Commission given by Jesus to his disciples to go, teach, and train
- Romans 15:20 – the need to go where Christ is not known
- James 1:27 – the command to care for orphans and widows.

Two of the elders are particularly passionate about global mission and regularly preach on the theme. This helps to ensure that it remains at the forefront of the church's agenda and that motivation remains high. The church is linked to a number of people and places around the world, of which the most significant is Uganda.

BFC partnership in Hoima, Western Uganda

BFC's involvement with Uganda started when a Ugandan pastor, Chris Komagum and his British wife, Heather, attended a mission prayer meeting at BFC in 1995. Chris spoke about the dire need for training in the rural churches of Uganda and put Ken and Sue in touch with a pastor in Western Uganda – Nicholas Kasaija. Nicholas was the leader of a group of churches in which the pastors were struggling in remote locations with poverty and lack of teaching, and were vulnerable to the advance of Islam and to cults and sects. Ken Matthews felt moved by their plight and in 1995 went out with Sue and others from the church for several weeks to provide discipleship training and ministry to the pastors.

That visit had a profound affect on Ken and Sue who felt a call on their church to get more involved with the Ugandans in practical ways as well as in further teaching and ministry. 'As we reflected on our trip and looked to how we might develop the link, we were very aware of the risk of us dominating the link culturally in ways that would be unhelpful and inappropriate. We also knew that simply throwing money at the needs in the area could create its own problems. Finally we decided to visit the indigenous leaders again the following year with the simple aim of getting to know them and understanding a little more of their situation. We spent a further two weeks in Uganda in 1996 and did no teaching or ministry but simply stayed with our Ugandan friends, building relationships and developing trust. Looking back, we now realise what a superb investment of time and resources that trip was, as the strong relationship which developed has been such a good foundation for what would follow.'

After this second visit the involvement of BFC in Hoima region has grown steadily, largely through regular visits by teams of about twelve BFC members led by Ken and Sue. Training in Bible teaching, ministry, health issues and leadership have remained a major element, and over six years at least thirty days' training was delivered to over seventy pastors in small groups. By 2002 BFC had begun to reduce their direct involvement in delivering training to the pastors and were handing over the responsibility, together with training materials, to selected Ugandan teachers.

In 1999, the relationship with the Hoima churches went through a difficult patch when a vocational training centre that BFC had funded was destroyed by a local 'king' who laid claim to the land on which it had been built. Even though this did not happen through any fault of the Ugandan Christians, they thought it would spell the end of the link with BFC. Despite the obvious distress such an event causes, BFC decided that their relationship with their friends in Uganda was too important to allow an unfortunate incident like this to get in the way.

At about the same time as this setback, Ken and Sue took three of their five children out to spend three months with Nicholas and his wife Betty and their church network in Hoima. While there they met a Christian head teacher called Geoffrey and felt drawn to support his vision of building a Christian secondary school. BFC managed to raise £58,000 for the project in 18 months from their own congregation and appeals to Trusts. Phase 1 of the school was completed in February 2002. Geoffrey understands BFC's concern to ensure full accountability for the money that they send to support the school and some sponsored orphans who attend it, and makes frequent contact by mobile phone, email and fax. Financial reports come every term along with letters from orphans. Ken and his team have spent many hours with the all-Christian staff and board of governors. Their aim is that the school will become completely self-financing, self-governing and self-propagating within five years through intensive input to training, shaping and linking with schools in the UK and in Uganda. These links are enabling the constitution and terms of reference for the school to be drawn up professionally through dialogue between the District Education Officer, two schools in the Bournemouth area led by heads from BFC and key leaders from the churches in Hoima.

Promoting self-support projects for pastors

'The abject poverty of so many of the pastors we got to know in Hoima was a real cause for concern to all of us who visited from BFC,' says Ken. 'The pastors were trying desperately to scratch a living and provide for their families, limiting the time they could spend on their church commitments and pastoral matters within their communities. We wanted to find ways of really helping the pastors without having them become dependent on us. Eventually we decided to help set up home-based projects which would provide support for the pastors and their families, church and community. The pastors were each encouraged to choose a project that they felt they could make work and were then given training in animal husbandry, crop farming, or whatever their chosen area was, to give the projects a good chance of success. We took up a collection at BFC and raised £2,800 which was handed over to a team of leaders who would make grants to the pastors for their chosen projects.

'The pastors were all expected to contribute to the cost of their training, helping them to gain a sense of ownership and commitment. Accounts for each project were drawn up and gifts directly to individuals were avoided. The aim right from the beginning was to give a hand up and not a hand out, working towards self-sustainability and self-governance as soon as possible.'

In 2002 a team from BFC visited ten of the projects established by the pastors and were amazed at their diversity and ingenuity, which were changing the lives of many for the better. Typical projects were: a brick works, a piggery, plantations producing pineapples, passion fruit, or bananas, animal husbandry (cows or goats), and chickens. A report to the church on one of the families they visited conveys vividly the transformation the project was helping to bring about in their standard of living

> Pastor Jackson, with his wife and six children, has been able to buy a cow, now pregnant. This provides milk for the children and will provide money for their education. Leading a church of 25 adults, he says he is able to serve them better because of this project. He also grows beans, and is building a church with the profits. They also stated that they would not lack the essentials now.

> This was an extremely poor family, whose situation was made more poignant by their generosity – Jackson bought five sodas for us. The children were clothed in rags, and the new baby, a week old, already looked ill. They welcomed us so kindly, but the poverty was shocking. These rural village people are at the wrong end of political, social and economic corruption ... This is where these projects are so successful. Money is transferred directly to the church, to people of integrity, where we know the money will be distributed fairly.

Not all that the visitors from Bournemouth brought to their friends in Uganda was planned. Ken and Sue often travelled as a family, which had an enormous influence on the family life of the pastors especially. One key leader when asked by a visitor 'so what have you learned from all this input?' replied, 'I now treat my wife as my best friend and enjoy my children.'

Northern Uganda

BFC has also been involved in supporting a church movement in the Lira area of Northern Uganda. The contact came about again through the wise counsel of Chris and Heather Komagum, who BFC say have saved them from many untrustworthy church contacts. The church movement in Northern Uganda is working in war-torn and deeply impoverished areas, due to invasions by the rebel Lord's Resistance Army and cattle rustlers. BFC and the movement have similar theological views and values, and BFC has given input into equipping the church leaders by means of intensive biblical training, leaders' forums, and exposition of basic Christian doctrine. The training is being cascaded through the movement, which has enjoyed phenomenal growth. Social concern has not been neglected here either. A member of BFC has led an extensive medical programme in consultation with the World Health Organisation, the local health authority and the church. Treating local people for bilharzia (a chronic illness caused by parasitic worms) and training some of them to deliver the treatment themselves is a major priority. At the time of writing already more than twenty thousand people have been treated. Education of leaders and families in remote rural settings has raised basic health care practice and enabled some prevention work to be carried out.

During 2002 and 2003 the area was severely blasted by rebel activity, which made BFC feel the need to intensify their mission trips for relief and encouragement of local churches. International agencies such as the World Food Programme predicted the worst humanitarian disaster that Northern Uganda has ever experienced in its disaster-ridden history. Despite this, and maybe even because of it, BFC members decided to continue visiting and as a result have forged phenomenal levels of partnership with the leadership team in Lira.

There are also plans to set up self-support projects in this area too, and BFC is shouldering the establishment of a Christian primary school, which will also house a clinic and health training unit. By February 2003 land was purchased and several classroom blocks had been built. The school is planned to be fully operational by June 2004 when Ken and the health team intend to spend an extended three-month trip living in Lira. During this time they plan to train teachers for the school and undertake an intensive course of training for local pastors. The health team is hoping to undertake training in remote villages.

Ken says: 'Involvement with remote, destitute and dangerous situations is not for the faint hearted – strong trust and relationship is founded upon standing with the suffering church in pain, in attack, in failure as well as success. These indigenous Christians live continuously in such conditions which we experience for short periods of time!'

Outreach to an Unreached People Group

Ken has long believed that outreach to Unreached People Groups (ethnically distinct groups which have had little or no contact with the gospel) is the principal calling for world mission on the church in our era. In the late nineties he and some other members of BFC took part in two days of prayer for such groups at the Wycliffe Bible Translators Centre in High Wycombe. 'We asked Wycliffe to suggest a UPG that BFC could adopt in East Africa, and they proposed a group where only one member was known to be a Christian. Simon Fry (another member of BFC) and I went to Nairobi to meet this man, Jimmy, who turned out to be very ill with hepatitis and about to drop out of college as a result. During our visit we asked God to confirm whether this link was right for BFC by healing Jimmy. After praying over him, Jimmy was immediately healed! In fact his healing was so complete that he worked through the night to catch up on course work! This miraculous answer to prayer was a tremendous encouragement both to us and to Jimmy and confirmed that it was right for us to continue to develop this link.'

Arrangements were made for Jimmy to come and spend three months in Bournemouth as a guest of the church. All parties were somewhat nervous about this, knowing that western materialism can ruin developing-world leaders. 'Normally it would have been an absolute no-no!' says Ken, 'but somehow God showed it to be essential.' In that time Jimmy got involved in church life, visited every cell group and became well known by the church members. They all came to love him, which meant that interest in his People Group became high and the link is well-supported. BFC is in touch with a church group in an area neighbouring the region where Jimmy's people live, with the aim of supporting church planting by those churches among his people. Their aim is to partner with indigenous churches in that region rather than trying to cross all the massive cultural barriers by attempting to do the church planting themselves. BFC has received a lot of support from Wycliffe in developing these plans and has found their guidance on these matters to be invaluable.

Lessons learnt

With all this experience of working with churches in other parts of the world, BFC can identify a number of lessons that they have learnt. Ken expresses these as follows:

1. 'The main reason why our partnerships have worked is that they are founded on strong personal relationships with people that we have grown to trust. Having Chris and Heather to advise and help us has been invaluable, not only to filter the many invitations to partner, but also to patch up teams who have suffered serious bouts of malaria, misunderstandings, extreme culture shock, armed robbery, dangerous travelling conditions and insecurity caused by rebel activities. The "filter" provided by Chris and Heather (their initial contacts in Western Uganda) has helped us to avoid many discouragements and pitfalls. The high quality of partners leading churches abroad has been the main key to "success". Extended periods spent residing as a family in the rural regions helped to build trust and to see cross-cultural obstacles more clearly. Together, leaders from the UK and Uganda have had to work through misunderstandings, annoyance, anger, sadness, and the problems of communicating the needs of situations to those struggling to build the home base in Bournemouth. Of course there have also been many times of great joy and cause for celebration too!

2. 'The transfer of money is a key area to get right. We have found that it is far better to give to projects led by teams of leaders, rather than to individuals. The economic imbalance between us in the UK and these pastors is so vast that individual gifts cause jealousies to emerge and relationships to be forced for all the wrong motives.

3. 'On one occasion we paid for a couple from East Africa to come to visit the church in Bournemouth. The visitors found it really hard to fathom the huge disparities in lifestyle between their own country and the UK, and thought that the British were so rich that we should be able to fund everything needed in their own country. It took a lot of work to undo the misconceptions, although

the relationships have now been rebuilt. These
difficulties have made us very wary of inward visits of
this kind, despite the successes of visits by people like
Jimmy.
4. 'The relationship in the north of Uganda has worked so
well because of the common biblical foundations and
the higher level of accountability necessary when
working in a team.'

Impact on BFC of the links with Uganda

By the end of 2002 around twenty of the members of BFC
had been out to Uganda. The ongoing relationship is very
exciting for the church. When asked to sum up what BFC
had gained from their involvement with Uganda, Ken
Matthews says: 'A major benefit is that it has given the
church a vision, and taken them outside their personal
problems. It is helping them to fulfil the prophetic mandate
of scriptures like Isaiah 58, and as a result is causing many
to respond to Christ just by visiting the church in
Bournemouth. The church members have in general a good
understanding of the gospel but struggle to take the harvest.
The problem in the Uganda churches is just the opposite.
Through partnering together both are being helped.

'The opportunity to make a difference knowing that the
money is finding its way directly to the problems on the
ground, without any being siphoned off, is very
stimulating. Also the generosity of the church and indeed
of local schools in Bournemouth has become outstanding.

'Our church members have learnt not to complain,
because they are so much better off materially than the
Ugandans. Visiting Uganda has caused some young
people to reconsider their future plans and vocations, and
certainly to think about how they use their resources. So

for example, one couple who were celebrating a wedding anniversary, and another who were getting married, asked for all gifts to be redirected into the orphan and school programmes. A number of young people have changed career direction to release time and skills to the mission teams and even to consider full-time mission in the future. All those who have visited have been very humbled to see how much is being achieved for God by Ugandan Christians who have so little materially.

'The links have also underlined how fleeting human life is in the light of eternity. Every time a team goes to Uganda they discover that one of the pastors we know has died, often from something really simple like a dental problem that could have been treated if basic medical care had been available in the area – and if he had been able to afford it.

'Undoubtedly BFC has been given spiritual life and the ability to take a harvest for Christ. In early 2003 people were responding to the gospel every week.'

4

The Lyndhurst Deanery

GLOBAL LINKS: *Rwanda*

CONGREGATION SIZE (2003): *This is a grouping of 16 churches of varying sizes*

DENOMINATION: *Anglican*

Companion Links

The worldwide Anglican Church is bound together by formal and informal links. Amongst these are the Companion Links under which every one of the 43 English dioceses now has links with at least one diocese or province in another part of the world. These links – some of which have been going for twenty years or more – have often started through personal relationships established when bishops from different countries have met together. Companion Links are supposed to work from a basis of equality and reciprocity, though this may be difficult when the material inequalities between two linked churches are very wide.

The nature and strength of these links vary widely because each diocese has organised and shaped its own links as it wished, and participation is voluntary at every level. Many links are now strong and valued by both sides.

The diocese of Winchester has Companion Links with several Anglican provinces in Africa, and each of its deaneries is responsible for maintaining links with one or more African diocese. The Lyndhurst Deanery, consisting of 16 parishes in and around the New Forest, has had a relationship with the Episcopal Church of Rwanda for around thirty years including the period of the 1994 genocide. Eleven of the parishes in the Deanery are linked to a parish or a diocese in Rwanda, and in some cases strong personal friendships have sprung up. For most of the churches in the Deanery, the Rwanda relationship is a significant focus of their mission interest and activity.

Early days

Although the links with Rwanda started in the mid-1970s, geographical distance and communication difficulties made it difficult for relationships to be meaningful. In 1992 three people from the Deanery visited with the aim of initiating closer ties between their parishes and their link churches in Rwanda. A second visit by four more visitors in 1994 sought to continue this process of relationship building. This second visit occurred only six weeks prior to the start of the genocide, and those who went recall a very evident atmosphere of tension and uncertainty. From the outbreak of the genocide until 1997, the Deanery's relationship with the Rwandan church was largely on hold because of the insecurity and total disruption to normal life.

Background on Rwanda

Rwanda, a country little bigger than Wales, was until 1962 administered by Belgium and 81 per cent of the 7.2 million population are at least nominally Christian. Of these 43 per cent are Roman Catholics, 10 per cent are Anglicans and the remaining 28 per cent are other denominations and groups. Disturbingly, this Christian majority did not prevent the worst African massacres of modern times.

The two predominant ethnic groups in Rwanda are the Tutsis and the Hutus, and the tensions between them have a long history. In 1994 extremists in the Hutu-led Government initiated the slaughter of Tutsis and moderate Hutus. More than 800,000 were killed while over two million fled to refugee camps in nearby countries.

The Deanery Missionary Committee decided to organise a visit in April 1999, and invited applications from members of churches in the Deanery. Thirteen people completed successful applications but it was decided that this was too big a group to send all at once; so five went on the April 1999 visit, followed by eight others in January 2000. Their brief was to stand alongside those recovering from the 1994 genocide, worship together, talk together, pray together and get to know one another better as they re-established the links.

April 1999: rebuilding and a setback

During the April 1999 visit, the relationship suffered another setback. The Deanery had undertaken a major fundraising drive for a building project in one of the Rwandan dioceses. This project had received a lot of publicity in Rwanda and was publicly backed by the Rwandan House of Bishops. At the end of their visit in 1999, the five visitors from the Deanery handed over to the bishop concerned half the sum raised. However, the advance publicity given to the project locally may have had unforeseen and serious consequences. Shortly after the handover ceremony, the bishop's accountant was shot and killed, and the bishop himself absconded with the money to the USA. Members of the Deanery later learnt that the bishop had been under considerable pressure from his local authority over building plans for the diocese. He may have felt frustrated and possibly frightened, especially after the death of his accountant, and succumbed to the temptation to leave the difficulties behind and use the money to establish a new life. The money was not recovered.

Obviously this was a huge disappointment to the New Forest churches that had worked hard to raise the money, and cast a cloud over prospects for any further fundraising for Rwanda. It could also have sabotaged the whole relationship. But once the dust had settled, the Deanery churches refused to let this deter them from continuing to build up links with the Rwandan church. They concluded that it had been a 'one-off' event involving human failure by one individual, and that in future it might be wiser if they provided 'seed money' for small specific projects only.

This decision was probably helped by the fact that, despite the unfortunate finale, the 1999 visit had a profound impact on those who went. After being formally welcomed by leaders of the Church of Rwanda they were taken on a tour of several dioceses. They had been warned that they could expect to be asked to preach, testify to their own relationship with Jesus, and to sing! And so they were. Almost everywhere they went they were greeted as VIPs by large crowds of singing and dancing children and adults, something that made the visitors rather uncomfortable. As so often when westerners visit Africa, they became acutely aware of the enormous gap in living standards and life expectations between themselves and the Rwandans. 'We were deeply impressed by their ability to make do with little, and to share with each other the little they had,' said Bridget, one of the group. 'The huge congregations at the Sunday services and the relaxed and exuberant style of worship, along with the Rwandan openness and readiness to talk about their faith, had a profound effect on us.'

The 1999 visit had long-term effects in the lives of all those who went. David Dale, a member of Marchwood Parish Church, was asked when he returned the following year to become the new commissary (or representative) of Shyogwe Diocese in Britain, and in April 2002 was ordained as Lay Canon there. David's experiences in Rwanda led directly to his training to become a lay reader in the Winchester Diocese. For another of the visitors, Tracy Masters, the Rwanda trip played a part in her decision to seek ordination. For a third visitor, Sandy White, the trip proved to be the first in what became a series of visits for charitable purposes to various countries of the world. Bridget Head, a fourth member of the group, felt her faith was both widened and deepened by the visit. She subsequently co-led a visit in 2002, and as Secretary to the Deanery Missionary committee has given talks on many occasions about Rwanda and the personal impact that visiting such a country can have. She has a boundless enthusiasm and love for the country and its people.

Nine months after the 1999 visit eight more people from five churches in the Deanery went on a three-week visit, which helped further in reinvigorating the relationship. Again, their main purpose was to reassure members of the Episcopal Church in Rwanda that they had not forgotten them and wanted to sit alongside and learn from and with them. They were also keen to visit the five Rwandan dioceses that had not been visited the previous year.

Trusting personal relationships

These trips gave most of the British visitors an opportunity to get to know personally some key people in the various dioceses and parishes to which they were linked, and to begin to identify those whom they thought could become trusted contacts for building an ongoing relationship.

Constantly improving international communication systems have also helped in developing and maintaining relationships, aided in particular by the establishment in the late nineties of a Rwandan mobile telephone network through American aid.

Deanery activity in support of the links

Prayer, fellowship and mutual support are important elements of the relationship with Rwanda. Much of the activity occurs at parish level on the British side, each parish relating to its Rwandan partner diocese or parish. But the Lyndhurst Deanery's Mission Committee provides the impetus, coordinates certain activities, and shares information on what parishes are doing, mainly through meetings held three or four times a year. For example, over the years the Committee has organised a scheme to sponsor orphans, another to send a container full of aid (five have been sent since 1994), and a Lent project in 2003 to buy 1,000 Bibles for Rwandan churches. They hold an annual Deanery week of prayer for Rwanda. The Mission Committee has a budget of around £1,000 per year, which is used to help pay for visits either to or from Rwanda.

Before each visit to Rwanda, several evenings of preparation are held, led by those who have been there before and by retired missionaries who have lived there. These meetings have been important in helping members of each group get to know each other and have prepared them to deal with cultural differences as well as issues of health and finance.

Parish activity: Hordle Parish Church

Hordle Parish Church, where Bridget Head is a member, has a lively relationship with the Rwandan Diocese of Butare and its cathedral. On a visit in 2002, Bridget and four others from the church spent some time in Butare. 'We were determined not to submit to the VIP treatment this time,' said Bridget, 'and to emphasise equality and partnership we insisted on working alongside the somewhat mystified Rwandans in building a compost heap and painting a school room!'

Before 1999, Hordle Parish Church had sent sums of money to Butare Diocese, but had often not received acknowledgement for the gifts or been confident that they had been used for the stated purposes. While cultural differences may have played their part in the Rwandan failure to account for such gifts, for a time the UK church had decided that it would be better to send goods rather than money. They sent several items in the containers organised by the Deanery to hospitals and schools in the diocese, together with musical instruments for use in the cathedral.

From about 2001 though, a number of factors combined to make this no longer an economic way of giving practical help, and they began to consider giving money once more. In 1999 and again on the 2002 visit, Bridget had met someone who she felt confident would handle any monetary gifts with integrity, so he became the person that they sent such money to. The approach they adopted was to fund relatively small, well-targeted projects, and to do all they could to satisfy themselves that the money was properly spent. Projects supported include the cathedral Sunday school, a new primary school nursery, re-roofing a local parish chapel and buying goats for individual members of the Mothers Union to give them an income-generating source for their families.

Communication between visits has often been a frustrating experience for the British churches, as letter-writing is not a normal part of traditional African culture. In recent years though, the advent of email and mobile phones offers hope of better two-way contacts for the future. 'During our trip in 2002 we decided that one way to ensure good communications with our key Rwandan contact was to take advantage of the new national phone network and buy him a mobile phone,' says Bridget. 'This has made a dramatic difference to maintenance of the relationship. It enables both sides to keep up to date with church and family news, to pray for each other, and to plan future joint activities. In addition it also means that when we send money we can make direct contact to check that it has arrived.'

Other churches in the Deanery are helping their linked Rwandan churches in varied ways, including child sponsorship, buying school supplies, supporting staff salaries and building projects. David Dale has set up a trust fund for Shyogwe Diocese which supports handicapped and disabled people, and water and agricultural projects.

Photographic evidence of any projects or work done in Rwanda with British help has proved of great value in giving practical reality to the links in the eyes of members of the churches of the Deanery. It is a real encouragement to church members if they can actually see where their gifts have been used, especially if the pictures have been taken by their own church members when visiting Rwanda.

Impact and aftermath of the genocide

No account of contacts with Rwanda since 1994 can ignore the devastating impact of the genocide. The group of five who went in 1999 had not been sure how to approach the matter. However they found their hosts wanted them to see some of the sites – often churches – where massacres had occurred and where, in many cases, the remains of those slaughtered still lay where they had fallen, preserved as gruesome memorials to what happened. Although stories of clergy and nuns who had encouraged the genocide were common in the British media in 1994 and after, the visitors now heard stories of courageous Hutu Christians who had sheltered and protected Tutsis from murderous mobs. In one parish, Hutu Christians who had ignored warnings to abandon their Tutsi friends were ruthlessly slaughtered beside them in the church. Such close contact with people who had been through so much trauma proved very moving and at times harrowing for the visitors. Many of those accused of involvement in the genocide were still imprisoned awaiting trial, but the visitors learnt of others, thought to have been involved, who were back living in the same villages as the families of those they were believed to have slaughtered.

The post-genocide Government of Rwanda is trying to rebuild the nation and bring reconciliation. Part of their strategy is to tackle the tribal mentality, which contributed so heavily to the genocide. The British visitors were not told the tribal background of any of the people they met in Rwanda. They are all called Rwandans, as the use of the terms 'Hutu' and 'Tutsi' is not allowed. Big efforts have been made to get the thousands of orphans left by the massacres adopted by families, often across tribal backgrounds. Church leaders and members have been generous in taking in such orphans. There is still an underlying tension within the church to events of the genocide, though often British visitors have become aware of this only as friendships deepen and Rwandans feel able to speak more openly.

The Episcopal Church of Rwanda has committed itself to supporting national reconciliation, and visitors from the Deanery have seen some of what they are doing for this purpose. A Rwandan Christian organisation called MOUCECORE, which receives support from the British charity Tearfund, aims to promote evangelism, reconciliation, counselling and community development, and runs practical programmes and workshops for pastors and laity in these matters. Another church-supported charity, SOLACE Ministries, offers spiritual, emotional, and practical support mainly to widows, orphans, families headed by children, and AIDS sufferers.

Two or three week visits are too short for British visitors to be able to grasp the full impact of the events of 1994. Those who went in 2002 thought that although the majority now wanted to move forward, many still remained traumatised. The loss of so many males, first through the genocide and now from the ongoing devastation of AIDS, also means that the economy and social structures will continue to suffer for many years to come. In consequence

aid and concern from the west are likely to be significant
for a long time yet. Bridget Head comments: 'We may have
just a small part to play in coming alongside the Episcopal
churches there. But it is very significant to them to know
that they are loved and cared for as Christian believers by
the rest of the Anglican Church.'

This belief that simple demonstration of interest and
concern is significant to Rwandan Christians is born out by
comments by Bishop Geoffrey Rwubusisi of the Diocese of
Cyangugu quoted in Mid-Africa Ministry News (January-
March 2003): 'We do not cry in Rwanda – it is a sign of
weakness. We swallow our pain – to talk about it hurts too
much . . . We are truly thankful for those who come and
show they care about us. We felt abandoned by the world
during the genocide, so it is good when people come and
hear our stories. We feel that the more they understand our
situation and are faithful in their prayers, the more we will
be comforted. We long to know true peace within our lives
and to live in harmony with our neighbours.'

Future plans

One or two individuals, such as David Dale, visit Rwanda
annually. In the summer of 2003 he planned to take a party
of teachers and clergy to Shyogwe Diocese to help train
Rwandan teachers. There were plans to invite two clergy
from Butare Diocese to visit Hordle in July 2003, and to
fund their fares and other expenses. Bridget says: 'We
believe that firsthand contact with Rwandans will help
British people get a different perspective on life.' A new
Rwandan theological college is being built and parishes in
the Deanery may be asked to sponsor individual students
who attend the college. Deanery members are being
encouraged to consider longer term service in Rwanda and

one teacher, Jenny Noyelle, has been accepted on the CMS (Church Mission Society) Share programme to work in Kigeme Diocese for two years.

Shared benefits

Despite setbacks, churches in the Lyndhurst Deanery remain deeply committed to their links with the Rwandan church. Summing up, the Reverend Malcolm Riches, Chair of the Deanery's Mission Committee, believes the benefits to the British churches involved are considerable and wide-ranging. He himself visited for the first time with the 2002 team. 'Living alongside and talking to Rwandans in their own country helped immensely with my understanding of their situation, their hopes and fears, and in appreciating their dedication to their Christian faith and to their congregations.

'Rwandans still generally feel they have much to learn from us about their faith and practice, but I'm sure that we learnt more from them – especially about what it means to stand up and talk about your beliefs. Their music and drama are often the main means of teaching both in school and church, since so few books are available. This has a vibrant and "up front" effect on their worship – something we need here in the UK too.

'From their perspective there is much to gain, quite apart from financial support. Their need to feel part of the world and not forgotten is very real. After the genocide they felt that no one was even interested in their plight, so the 1999 visitors had a bit of answering to do when they arrived. But nevertheless all those they met were so pleased that they were there at all. We have always felt incredibly warmly welcomed and at home in Rwanda – they are extremely hospitable. Language has never been a problem – their second language is French and their third language is English – which many speak. Otherwise it's sign language!

'It is surely our Christian responsibility to have a wider vision than just our parish or even our own diocese – and these links have often surprised us and widened our experiences enormously over the years.'

5

Mexborough Wesleyan Reform Church, Yorkshire

GLOBAL LINKS: *Lithuania and the Ukraine*

CONGREGATION SIZE (2003): *about 85*

DENOMINATION: *Wesleyan Reform*

Mexborough in South Yorkshire, between Sheffield and Doncaster, is the mining equivalent of a small market town. Though there were never any coal pits in Mexborough itself, at one time there were probably around twenty-five pits in the immediate area, with a power station at one end of the town and the largest coking plant in Europe at the other. All of that has gone and for years the town has suffered great deprivation. In the early 1990s one housing estate recorded 91 per cent unemployment. Some new employment has come into the area but not enough to regenerate the local economy.

The Wesleyan Reform denomination was founded over one hundred and fifty years ago as a breakaway from

Methodism, and is now a small group of churches with around two thousand members. The Mexborough church is, in reality, a group of four small churches that pool resources and share a common leadership. The church is strong on community and has a generous attitude, opening its heart and pockets to meet needs. It has a strong emphasis on systematic, expository preaching and its worship is very much in the charismatic vein with excellent musical accompaniment.

The all-age congregation is a representative cross-section of the local community but has a higher proportion of school teachers and immigrants than the neighbourhood around it. Financially, there are a few members who are relatively well off for the area, but the majority are council tenants.

The start of a relationship

David Mills joined the leadership team of the church in 1985, after spending nearly twenty years in mission work in Ghana. In the early nineties his wife Margaret was secretary to Steve Timmis, the director of Radstock Ministries.

Radstock Ministries

Radstock exists to help local churches become directly involved in mission. Opportunities range from summer mission teams and short-term placements to training pastors, sending workers, and providing support for drug rehabilitation and children's workers. They will work with churches of any size. See the end of this book for information on how they work, and how to contact them.

In 1993 David and Margaret were asked by Radstock to go to the Baltic States in order to assess the church situation and the prospects for setting up church-to-church partnerships. Most of their time on that visit was spent in Latvia, but they also attended a meeting of church leaders in Lithuania. The atmosphere at that meeting was quite discouraging, because the churches seemed to have so many problems. However one of those present – the President of the Union of Pentecostal Churches in Lithuania – said that their experience in Lithuania was much more positive, and that they were seeing a number of young men emerging into church leadership.

'We met a young man of twenty-three – Ramunas, who was pastoring a Pentecostal church in the Lithuanian city of Panevezys,' David recollects. 'He and I struck up a good relationship, and I promised to visit him if ever I came back to the Baltics. To my surprise, a year later I received an invitation from Ramunas to spend two weeks in August with him and his church in Panevezys, and decided to go. Margaret and I found a church with 150 members, most of whom were young. The 23-year-old pastor, who had only had six months at Bible College, felt the need for a father-figure to give him guidance, and during the visit I did my best to provide encouragement and counsel. We looked together at how to deal with pastoral problems, pressures from churches that seemed heretical, passages of Scripture that needed exploring and the development of discipleship training.'

During that visit David also met a young member of the church called Richard Rickus, who had been given a bursary to attend Northumbria Bible College but had no money for his travel or living expenses, no other contacts in Britain, and nowhere to go for his vacations between the college terms. When David mentioned Richard's predicament to the church on his return to Mexborough, the congregation wanted to help him. David continued: 'They therefore undertook to fund his fares and his living expenses in the UK for a year, and to give him accommodation during the vacations. In fact Richard did so well at Bible College that one year's study turned to three, and was then topped off by a fourth year at All Nations Christian College to turn his diploma into a degree. Our church funded him throughout this period. Richard has since been working at the Lithuanian Embassy in London, assisting the Ambassador.'

Through this personal link with Richard, interest in the Baltics became high in the Mexborough church. In about 1995 a member of the church who was a teacher opened an 'English Language School' in the town for Christians from the Baltics who wanted to learn, or improve, their English. The school ran on a charitable basis and not as a money-making venture. There were never more than one or two students at a time, and most stayed for about six months. They were given tuition free of charge and free accommodation by members of the congregation. Several close friendships were built up as a result of church members hosting students. In one case a translator was invited to her English friend's wedding. In another case, a young Englishwoman who had paid two visits to Lithuania (the second for two months to help in an orphanage) wanted a special kind of Lithuanian wedding cake. The cake was duly purchased and flown to England for the wedding.

Past students from the Mexborough English Language School are now involved in a variety of jobs. One of the first two people to attend the school is now a translator in Vilnius Theological College. David and Margaret were very glad of her services in March 2003 as she interpreted their lectures on Marriage and the Christian Family. She has also tasted 'missionary service' in Tatarstan when she went there on interpretation business. A student from Estonia is now married with a family and is working in her local church. One student from Latvia was able to progress from being a cook to being the Welfare for Families in Need coordinator of Hope for the Children, an agency working with street children in Riga. Another has used his English to get a job with an airline at the airport in Riga to support himself, while also pastoring a church in a town some distance away. Another is a house-parent in Riga caring for her 'family' of six ex-street children. The most recent student was, in 2003, completing her Masters in Mission – despite having had no English when she arrived in the UK four years earlier – and considering where God wanted her to serve.

Regular visits have also taken place from Mexborough to the Baltics. Since 1993 teams ranging in age from sixteen to sixty-one have gone out at least every other year for visits usually lasting two weeks. They link up with a local church and build friendships in the first week, then in the second week they and the local church members work together doing street evangelism, working in Government-run youth camps, and visiting orphanages. Some teams have been involved in camps for teaching English where Bible studies and songs in English are a major part of the programme.

In 1997 a lady named Helen from the church went to work with Hope for the Children in Riga. Although her initial commitment was just for a fortnight's holiday, she returned for another 'holiday' six months later and became so committed to the work and the place that she moved to Riga. She later sold her home in Mexborough to enable her to buy a house in Riga where she could give a home to the older children from the streets.

David himself visits regularly and provides teaching and guidance to young church leaders. 'I am usually based at The Church of the Living God in Panevezys, which is in good standing with other churches in the town. These churches join in whatever programme is arranged, and so do churches in surrounding towns and villages, some of which are "plants" from the Church of the Living God. On one occasion, I spoke at a church gathering in Panevezys about giving, having discerned a "poverty spirit" in the church there. It was easy to understand why there was such a feeling among the Christians: they had become much poorer during the declining years of Soviet rule and many were not being paid. The congregation and a group of church leaders took this teaching so much to heart, that the next time I visited they took up a collection of money for me to take to a congregation in India which I visit from time to time. I was particularly moved when one widow gave me a single dollar note that she had had for years. That dollar travelled safely to India and I eventually passed it to an Indian widow who was greatly in need. Although the Lithuanian congregation are far from rich, they realised that they were wealthy in comparison with those in India.'

Money has not been a major element of the relationship, but the Mexborough church has provided targeted funding for specific projects. They gave money towards the purchase of a minibus for the church and helped a young pastor to buy an apartment for himself and his family in the area where he was trying to plant a church. Other sums of money have gone to Hope for the Children to enable the children to have a holiday in the summer. One year an airline allowed the children to travel to the UK for 10 per cent of the usual fare and so about fifteen children arrived in South Yorkshire and were shown the delights of the area including a visit to the American Adventure Theme Park!

Other mission links

The links with Ghana and India mentioned earlier are primarily a personal link of David's, stemming from his time in mission in Ghana and mission visits to India. But in addition to their lively links with the Baltics, the Mexborough church has also developed a partnership with a church in Benin. Recently they provided seed funding for an agricultural project, which they hope will provide an ongoing income for evangelism in the area of their partner church.

By 2002, 57 of the church's members had been to one of their linked churches for at least a week, and some twenty-three foreign visitors from the Baltics, India or Ghana had spent at least three months in Mexborough.

Lessons learnt by the Mexborough Church through the link with the Baltics

'Perhaps the main lesson that we have learnt has been that people without "platform ministries" can do a tremendous amount in mission,' says David. 'Because of the youthfulness of most of the Pentecostal congregations and their pastors in the Baltics, mature western Christians who are prepared to befriend them can have a vital role to play. One lady in her sixties went in the late nineties as a member of what was supposed to be a "youth team" to Lithuania, and proved to have such a ministry of encouragement that the church there has regularly invited her back ever since. She now goes for three to six months at a time, to live in the community and relate in a natural, supportive way with the church members.

'The church has come to see that mission is multi-faceted, and that a very good way to get involved is to invest "holidays" in mission enterprise – provided that it is done with cultural sensitivity.

'Important lessons that were learnt, sometimes the hard way, include the need to avoid presuppositions about the perceived needs of the people you work with, to comply with local customs and laws, and that there is a desperate need for long-term, relational ministry that is modest in promises but abundant in delivery.'

6

St John's, Blackheath

GLOBAL LINKS: *Tanzania*

CONGREGATION SIZE (2003): *about 250*

DENOMINATION: *Anglican*

The congregation at St John's Church in Blackheath, South-East London, includes many with professional skills and high incomes, reflecting the affluence of the local area. Until the mid nineties the church's involvement in global mission mainly consisted of tithing their total income and allocating the resulting amount between various mission agencies. This was dutifully done each year, but actual interest in global mission was hard to sustain.

The beginnings of a partnership

In the early 1990s St John's embarked on a project to improve and renovate their church buildings and by 1994 had raised

£400,000. At this stage they decided that they would give 10 per cent of the money raised to church building projects in developing countries. They felt it was wrong to spend all that money on their own church building, when Christians in developing countries struggled to raise the money for their own places of worship. Finding a suitable building project was not easy. In fact they had started to give the money to other Christian groups in the UK, when Pastor Hilkiah Omindo, a parish priest from the (Anglican) Diocese of Mara in Tanzania who was studying theology in London, visited St John's and made a very convincing presentation to the church council. He had heard of the tithe fund from a retired missionary to Tanzania who had moved to Blackheath. He told the church council of his vision for a new cathedral for his diocese to be built on the shores of Lake Victoria. Coincidentally the church building which was then serving as the cathedral in Musoma was also called St John's.

St John's, Blackheath thought this might be the project for them. But because the Diocese of Mara was linked – through the Anglican Communion's Companion Links – to the English Diocese of Wakefield, they first made inquiries to establish whether they would be treading on any toes there if they took on the project themselves. Having learnt that Wakefield were happy for St John's to get involved, the church leaders sent Graham McClure, a member of the church council, to Musoma in December 1994 as a guest at the installation of Hilkiah Omindo as Bishop of Mara Diocese. He was also tasked to assess the viability of the project and how St John's could best get involved.

'Life in Musoma provides a stark contrast to the comfortable London suburb that I was used to,' says Graham. 'Tanzania is one of the most impoverished countries in the world and the village people I visited were desperately poor. The country was just emerging from a long period in which the economy had been centrally directed, under a regime that had not encouraged private enterprise. Many Tanzanians I met seemed to have little motivation to better themselves and their communities, and no awareness of business procedures. I was also dismayed to see that local building skills were of a low order and realised that if the cathedral-building project were to work, the Tanzanians needed more than just a transfer of funds. They also needed a transfer of building and financial management skills – and these were skills that St John's congregation had in abundance.

'Although many Tanzanians in the area were Christians, they were mostly only first-generation believers, and the animist beliefs and traditional practices of their culture still had a strong influence. They needed Bible-based teaching to help strengthen them in their faith and practical Christian living.'

Transferring skills as well as money

In the light of Graham's report and recommendations, the church embarked on a skill-sharing partnership with the Diocese of Mara, working closely with the bishop himself who proved to be a man of vision, courage, integrity and insight. Members of St John's with skills in architecture, construction and financial management helped throughout the planning and construction of the cathedral, which began in 1996. Teams from the church visited periodically, but they needed someone on the ground to keep track of the project for them. They found such a person in Andrew Maclean, a Crosslinks missionary based in Tanzania, who took on this responsibility as a hobby, supervising the work on his lunch breaks, weekends and at holiday times.

The project was just getting under way when Mike Marshall joined St John's as the new vicar. When he learnt of the level of involvement proposed by the church, he was at first deeply anxious about the wisdom of the undertaking. However as he came to realise the wealth of relevant skills in St John's, and how easy it was to travel to and from Tanzania, he revised his earlier opinion and became an enthusiastic supporter of the whole scheme. He himself went on one of the church work parties that go to Tanzania, normally on an annual basis. Mike is now thrilled at the direct link with Christians in Musoma and is keen to encourage others to consider this direct church-to-church link.

As the involvement in Tanzania started to gather pace, so St John's perceptions of what could be achieved began to grow. Having realised from Graham's initial report that there was a lot that they as a congregation could contribute practically as well as financially, in consultation with Bishop Hilkiah they developed plans to transfer skills and boost the local economy for the longer term. In particular they worked with the diocese's vocational training centre to introduce courses and provide training in a range of building processes such as concrete roof tile and block manufacturing, and joinery. These not only ensured that the cathedral was built to a higher standard than would otherwise have been possible without importing skilled labour and manufactured parts from outside, but also gave local people skills that would enable them to earn more in the future.

Altogether St John's transferred £75,000 as a contribution to the cost of building the cathedral. The Diocese of Wakefield very generously contributed over £22,000 and the local church raised an astonishing £20,000 themselves. The cathedral was completed in 2000 and opened that October by the Tanzanian Justice Minister. It is believed to be the largest locally built construction in Northern Tanzania, and has seating for 2,500 people.

The expanding vision

By 2000, St John's involvement in Musoma and district consisted of far more than a building project. Through regular visits in which they made friendships with local people and observed their daily lives and struggles, the people of St John's became more and more committed to working with the church and the people in that area, and thought up some varied and innovative projects.

Perhaps the most innovative idea is the 'twinning' arrangement they have set up with a hill village near Lake Victoria. The overall aim is to enable the villagers to become self-sufficient through improving their subsistence agriculture, by growing cash crops and developing micro-enterprises. For this purpose, and with funding supplied by the members of St John's and the Blackheath community, a range of small projects has been started for the village. These include

- Forming an agricultural co-operative of ten farmers who were trained in forestry and other skills at the diocese's agricultural training centre, and equipped at an investment of £5,000 overall. (The farmers in the co-operative have agreed to repay St John's funding within five to ten years, so that more farmers can be helped)
- Sponsoring a child's education for a year
- Planting trees
- Supplying Irish high-yield milk goats
- Building the pastor a house
- Digging a well and providing a water tank.

The £4,000 funding for these projects was raised without difficulty within St John's by selling the schemes in small 'packages' as Christmas or Easter presents within the church and local community: for example 'plant a tree for

50p', 'sponsor a child's education for a year', or 'buy an Irish milk goat'.

Graham and the Tanzania team at St John's believe that the 'twinning' model they have developed could be taken up by other churches wanting to show practical Christian love through promoting wealth-creation and self-sufficiency in communities in Africa. They would be delighted if churches elsewhere in the UK caught the vision. St John's could help to establish a link through Bishop Hilkiah and offer the benefit of their experience. See contact details at the end of this chapter.

In addition to this ongoing 'developmental' work, special appeals are sometimes made at St John's for money to send to Musoma for particular problems such as harvest failures, destitute widows, to provide equipment for farms, etc.

Relationships at the heart of partnership

The strong relationship between the leaders of St John's on the one hand, and Bishop Hilkiah and two of his staff on the other, has been crucial in the successful growth of this partnership. St John's members have felt able to fully trust these Tanzanians (one of whom sadly died in 2001), and are confident that any money they send will be used for the intended purpose.

This is how Graham explains the process for developing new projects: 'New projects may be thought up either by the bishop and his staff, or by the St John's Tanzania Committee. Decisions on which ones are most likely to succeed are arrived at jointly. Such projects are not imposed on the people or the villages. Any proposal that diocesan officials and St John's members think are viable are put to the villagers concerned for them to discuss and approve – or reject. Thereafter, liaison takes place with the village headman. Tanzanian villagers have a different approach towards leaders in their society from that of Europeans. They are more deferential, and can sometimes be slow to air their reservations and criticisms about initiatives brought in from outside. It takes time to build up relationships of trust and openness. The diocesan officials are of course a great link between the two cultures.'

Members of St John's, Blackheath now make at least one visit a year to their friends in Musoma. Members of other churches have started to come along too, and sometimes the group can be 20-strong. All the trips have a practical emphasis and involve some kind of building, but Bible teaching and youth work are also often incorporated. In 2003, for instance, they planned to build water tanks for poor farmers, 'modern' squatting toilets to replace holes in the ground, and goat sheds. Graham McClure comments: 'The culture shock is high for many who come with us for the first time, and they sometimes have difficulty in understanding why some western ways of dressing are not suitable in Tanzania and give very much the wrong signals. Tanzanian greetings are initially hard to grasp, and have caused some embarrassing moments. The Tanzanian words for goat and nurse are very similar!

'While the Europeans have financial and educational advantages compared to the villagers they work with, after two weeks living in a Tanzanian village there is no way they can feel superior. For a start, the Tanzanians work five times harder. They are attuned to living in the bush; they have fewer hang-ups and neuroses than the Europeans, and are generally much happier people.'

Not all sweetness and light!

As with any cross-cultural partnership, the people of St John's have learnt to cope with disappointments, setbacks, cultural misunderstandings, and health hazards. Begging letters from individual Tanzanians addressed to individuals in Blackheath are quite common, and can cause distress to those who receive them. Mike, the vicar, and the Tanzania Committee have issued firm advice that money should not be sent in response to such letters, but the stories can be very sad and some recipients have found it hard to resist.

'AIDS is the largely unmentioned spectre that stalks this area of Tanzania along with much of the rest of sub-Saharan Africa,' reflects Graham. 'It is common for young and apparently healthy Tanzanians to sicken and die quite suddenly, but the probable cause is almost never mentioned in the church. The diocese runs an AIDS education scheme which was set up by a Crosslinks missionary, Caroline Maclean. In 2003, St John's is sending out a doctor and nurse to assess the medical needs of the area and try and set up a five-year plan to help with health issues.'

A two-way process

'Firsthand experience of another culture is nearly always beneficial,' Mike believes. 'But those who have gone to Tanzania have been touched at a deeper, spiritual, level. Life expectancy for villagers is only forty-five and their lives are very hard, but visitors from St John's have been profoundly moved by the cheerfulness and faith shown by Tanzanian Christians. It has helped them to see the materialism of western society in a new and unfavourable light.

'One year, we were unable to find a suitable date for the local diocesan bishop to preside at our confirmation service. Our bishop agreed to invite Bishop Hilkiah instead, but as he couldn't come, he recommended Bishop Gerard from Western Tanzania as an alternative. Bishop Gerard came, and his presence and contribution made the service very different and enriching for all of us. We took a collection during the service and raised enough money to pay for the bishop's return fare. This was a wonderful experience for us and I would like to encourage more visits like this from Tanzania.'

Mike and members of the congregation have also seen evidence that St John's practical involvement in Tanzania has been noticed by the local Blackheath community, and has given the church added credibility. Many people outside the church have generously contributed to the various small schemes in Tanzania.

'Thinking back to those early contacts, and the presentation that Bishop Hilkiah made at the St John's church leaders' meeting in 1994, no one knew then the significance of that first meeting,' reflects Graham. 'The relationship between the two groups of Christians has grown and grown. Both have benefited enormously from being linked together in their work in the diocese. The Tanzanians have a wonderful new church which glorifies God, and they also now have a group of tradesmen who can build low-cost high-quality buildings. Some villagers now have access to fresh water for the first time in their lives and are building economical viability into their lives, and a lot of children have access to education for the first time.

'Those of us who have been out there no longer take for granted the ability to turn on the tap and find fresh water coming out. We have visited some of the most spectacularly beautiful scenery in the world, and have met and formed friendships with wonderful people who trust God in a way that seems to be beyond many of us in the west. For us, a year without a trip to Tanzania is a year with something missing.'

Mike and the Tanzania Committee have big plans for their links with Tanzania. As well as inviting members of other churches and even members of the general public to come and share the experience, their plans include

- Extending the number of trips to two a year
- Helping other churches twin with a Tanzanian village through the Diocese of Mara`s agricultural training scheme
- Pumping water from the lake to irrigate the plateau of Nyankanga
- Extending the number of farmers in the co-operative to create a strong economic unit
- Helping with the medical needs of the area
- Organising the first 7-a-side Rugby tournament in Northern Tanzania!

If you are interested in twinning with a Tanzanian village as St John's has done, you can contact Graham McClure by email on: grahammcclure@hotmail.com for information and advice to get you started. Alternatively you could write to him c/o St John's Church Office, Stratheden Road, Blackheath, London SE3 7TH.

7

Altrincham Baptist Church, Manchester

GLOBAL LINKS: *Uganda*

CONGREGATION SIZE (2003): *up to 1,000*

DENOMINATION: *Baptist*

Altrincham is a pleasant suburb of Manchester in the Metropolitan Borough of Trafford. Altrincham Baptist Church (ABC) has about four hundred and fifty members, up to 1,000 attendees on a Sunday, and an annual budget in excess of £400,000 – 20 per cent of which is allocated to mission. The £80,000 raised annually for mission is used to support a large number of people and agencies engaged in mission in mainly traditional ways. Since 1999, however, the church has developed a growing link with Christians in the Ugandan town of Jinja, which has developed in some surprising directions.

During the 1990s a Ugandan dance and drama group called Heartsong toured the UK and on several occasions came to Manchester. Roger Sutton, now ABC's senior pastor, and members of the congregation began to build friendships with the group and especially with the leader Sam Kasango. Sam regularly invited Roger to visit Uganda, but at that time Roger had no real inclination to take Sam up on his offer.

In 1998 during a Sunday service Roger heard God tell him: 'Go to Uganda and take a team' but he forgot about it. Then about eighteen months later the Lord said to him: 'Why haven't you gone?' and he felt rebuked. He knew he had to take action but had little idea what was involved in taking a group to Uganda. He consulted a couple in his congregation who were members of Soapbox, which sends out teams worldwide, including to Africa, and also took advice from the African Pastors' Fellowship. As a result he decided to do a ten day preparatory trip in October 1999 before leading the first team of 21 in February 2000. The destination they chose was Jinja where they linked up with Jinja Christian Centre (JCC), a church founded by Sam Kasango. They chose to work with Sam because of their existing relationship with him and the trust that had grown between them. At that early stage they were far from clear about what they should be doing but went to explore possibilities. During that first trip they undertook a mixture of ministry and practical work, and held a conference for pastors.

As members of a Baptist church, the visitors from Altrincham also made contact with a local Baptist church in Jinja. There was some tension here, however, as the Jinja church was strongly influenced by American Southern Baptist missionaries who did not agree with Roger's teaching on the gifts of the Spirit. But the church had a concern to help orphaned children in the area, and ABC showed interest in helping them with their project.

On the team's return to Manchester a couple of church members, Paul and Jan Spooner, began to take a lead within ABC in developing the Jinja links and eventually a Uganda Core Team was established. Because Roger had been involved it placed the issue of Uganda at the heart of the church, and he retained a keen interest.

From his first visit, Roger and the ABC leadership took the view that money could not be left out of the relationship because of the huge inequalities between the UK and Uganda. ABC's thinking on the issue was heavily influenced by Acts 4:32-35, which states that the believers 'shared everything they had . . . There were no needy persons among them.' They were aware of the likelihood that they would receive requests from individuals for money, and before the first team went out guidelines were suggested on how to respond to such requests – although sticking to them was not easy when faced with extreme human need.

Team members were advised to explain that they were part of a church team which was providing financial support from central funds directly to Ugandan organisations, not to individuals. This was exactly what was happening in practice, but many team members also ended up making personal gifts before the trip was over, not because they felt pressurised, but because they genuinely wanted to.

Which project to support?

In February 2001 a 15-member team went out to Jinja, again preceded by a preparatory field trip a few months earlier. The ABC team was now more focused on specific projects, and had already supported the local Baptist church financially with the purchase of a plot of land to build a vocational training centre for disadvantaged children. However during the 2001 trip it became clear to the ABC team that the Baptist church in Jinja did not have a well-developed sense of their vision or how to achieve it. Their priorities for the proposed centre (such as a very top-heavy administrative structure) were not the same as ABC's and the location of the chosen plot of land, several kilometres from the church, did not seem ideal. Despite the fact that ABC had not made any commitment to ongoing financial support for the project beyond the initial purchase of the land, and ABC members had stated this clearly on several occasions, it was evident that the Jinja church were expecting them to provide significant further funding. ABC felt increasing misgivings.

During the course of 2001, Jinja Christian Centre expressed interest in getting involved in the training of orphans and other needy children, and for a while the ABC team thought the ideal solution would be for the two churches to cooperate with ABC on a joint project. They tried to bring them together, and thought that an understanding existed between the three churches involved, but when a team next went from ABC in February 2002, it quickly became clear that in practice the two Ugandan churches would not be able to work together effectively. It seemed that Uganda was no different from the UK in terms of denominational differences. Even ideas would not be easily shared, let alone a project with property.

A few of those who went on the 2001 team had visited the Nile Vocational Institute (NVI), situated on the outskirts of Jinja on the opposite side of the River Nile. It had been started in 1988 by the African Evangelistic Enterprise, a Christian-led organisation. In 2002 the entire Core Team visited it, and found an impressive and fully functional centre with accommodation and dining facilities, offering an extensive range of training courses and capable of providing vocational training for up to six hundred orphans and other disadvantaged Ugandan young people. NVI also had spare capacity, as it only had 375 students in attendance. After discussions with the director and other staff, the ABC team concluded that the best way that they could help AIDS orphans and other young people was to sponsor students at the existing facilities at NVI.

The ABC team then invited both the Jinja Baptist Church and JCC to nominate children whom ABC could sponsor at NVI. While JCC were happy to be involved, the Baptist church leaders made plain their bitter disappointment that ABC would not be supporting their own building project. The ABC members later learnt that if a Ugandan makes a financial need known to a westerner and the latter shows concern or a willingness to pray about it, the Ugandan sees this as a firm undertaking to meet the need.

UgandAid

On their return to the UK, the Uganda Core Team took the decision to immediately sponsor six children at NVI out of existing funds, and asked NVI to contact both JCC and the Baptist church to ask for nominations to fill three places each.

The next twelve months witnessed the remarkable development of UgandAid, a sponsorship scheme that aims to place as many as seventy-five children per year on three-year courses at NVI, effectively taking the establishment to its full capacity.

The team that visited Uganda in February 2003 included members of Farnham Baptist Church, and St Brides, an Anglican church in Old Trafford, both UgandAid supporters. The team were able to meet some of the 51 young people that are already placed at NVI as a direct result of UgandAid, and it was an emotional experience for those that had been involved in setting up and developing the scheme.

As one of the Uganda Core Team members expressed it: 'Some of the youngsters there had never met these white people who, they were told, were responsible for them being at NVI; their faces showed shyness and a lack of understanding, confusion even. "How could this be?" Others were beaming with joy and appreciation. I have never found any experience in my life to be, at the same time, as humbling and rewarding as that moment.'

Jinja Christian Centre and the Baptist church now each have 16 students enrolled at NVI. The speed with which this has happened has caused the Baptist church to review its attitude to the difficult decision that was taken by ABC the previous year. 'You must allow an African to change his mind about something' was how their pastor put it.

The UgandAid scheme is being promoted by Trafford Council, and has featured in local press and radio items. The sponsorship base has already spread significantly outside ABC into Trafford and beyond.

Whilst child sponsorship support is focused on individuals and groups, future UgandAid plans include the establishment of a Motor Vehicle Mechanics building and training course at NVI, the funding for which it is hoped will come from the corporate sector. At the same time, Jinja Christian Centre and the Baptist church are both being encouraged to contribute towards the scheme.

Jealousies within a denomination

'From our experience in Uganda,' Roger said, 'jealousies can easily be created when one church within a denomination has a relationship with a western church through which it receives money or other benefits. This is something that other UK churches contemplating a link need to be aware of.'

Other projects emerge

The UgandAid scheme was far from being the only project which emerged from these visits, though it was the most significant and high profile, and has attracted support from across the church congregation and local community. The Ugandan link soon began to spread much wider than just ABC and its immediate community, in a way that was quite unplanned by Roger and the ABC Uganda Core Team. They now recognise three broad streams of activity: Personal callings, ABC calling and Trafford Association calling.

Personal callings

A number of people have felt called to use their skills to establish individual projects, mainly humanitarian in nature, to aid groups or small communities in the Jinja area. The schemes extend from preventative medical training and hospital nurses training, to car mechanics, road safety training and adult literacy. Much of the activity connected with these schemes occurs during what is now established as the 'annual visit' from ABC, although since 2002 supplementary small team visits have increasingly been taking place.

One ABC member, Dr Jan Webb, who has now visited Uganda on three occasions, has received an award from the Royal College of General Practitioners in recognition of her pioneering work establishing a village-based preventative health care programme with the Ugandan organisation Arise Africa.

Whilst the February 2002 team members were involved in, amongst other things, delivering basic preventative health care training, the 2003 team invested much time, energy and money in the refurbishment of a disused building at Jinja Hospital. The newly created 'Hospital Educational Training Centre' will be used by Sue Johnson, a Nursing Administrator and member of Farnham Baptist Church, and others throughout the year, to deliver a nurses' training programme Sue established with the hospital management following three visits to Uganda in the previous 12 months.

Act4Africa is a newly formed charity, and is now an associate ministry that has grown out of the ABC trips. Kathy Smedley, a teacher, visited Uganda in February 2000. Her actor husband Martin joined the 2001 trip. Together they formulated the idea of using drama, something that really stimulates the Ugandan people, in order to deliver an important AIDS awareness message. Since 2001, drama-training workshops in Manchester have been followed by two weeks of practical application in Uganda, working with Ugandan friends from JCC. Their work is independent of the other ABC Ugandan activities, and may soon be extended into Tanzania.

As a result of taking part in successive visits to Jinja, one member of the congregation felt called to full-time mission work in Uganda, and ABC approached BMS (Baptist Missionary Society) to ask them to send her. Although BMS at that time did not operate in Uganda, after consideration they agreed to start work there. After completing the necessary BMS training programme, she is now working with the Baptist Union of Uganda for BMS.

The Uganda Core Team sees its role as to facilitate and support these 'Personal Calling' activities, and to provide general oversight. Loose guidelines have been drawn up to enable each 'activity leader' to operate and make decisions within the broad areas of delegated authority. The leaders themselves and not ABC are responsible for their own fundraising but the church does account for the money raised within its Uganda Fund.

ABC's corporate calling

There are some projects which are directly under the guidance of an ABC pastor or other church leaders and may be funded – at least partly – from the ABC mission budget. One is the formalisation of the link between ABC and Jinja Christian Centre whereby ABC provides some significant core funding to JCC. This is a similar arrangement to that which exists between ABC and a church in Pecel, Hungary, to which ABC has also sent teams in recent years.

Practical support for the Baptist Union of Uganda and some of the Ugandan pastors is a developing part of ABC's corporate involvement.

Civic links

While on the visit to Jinja in February 2001, Roger met the Mayor of Jinja who expressed a wish to 'twin' with Altrincham's borough, Trafford. A few weeks later, Roger happened to meet the Mayor-to-be of Trafford at a party, mentioned this idea to him and was surprised to find him enthusiastic at the prospect, even though Trafford had refused to enter into any twinning arrangements in the past. The Mayor arranged for Roger to meet with the leader of the council and the Chief Executive to discuss the issue, and good relationships were established which enabled the idea of a 'friendship link' with Jinja to be taken further.

The culmination was that on the third big trip to Jinja, in February 2002, 23 members of the church, plus four from other churches, were accompanied by the Mayor of Trafford and a member of his senior staff plus two members of the Mayor's local community.

The formal signing of the friendship agreement between the people of Trafford and Jinja took place in the Jinja Municipality Council Chamber, and was widely reported on Ugandan TV, radio and in the press. Mayor Harry Faulkner was clearly touched by his experience of Uganda, saying one evening that 'this has been the best day of my life.'

The friendship agreement states that its objective is to 'purposely develop friendship to increase mutual learning and support in areas of environment conservation, tourism, human resource, culture and education for the benefit of both communities'.

A Trafford-Jinja Association has been set up, involving Trafford Council, ABC and St Brides Anglican Church in Stretford, a less wealthy area of the borough. The purpose of the Association is 'to guide and support Trafford residents, businesses and other groups and organisations to fulfil the commitment set out in the Trafford-Jinja Friendship Agreement'. The Association is in the process of applying for grant aid to finance the appointment of a Development Officer but, significantly, the ongoing work and activity in Uganda is not reliant on this financial support.

The relationships that have been established between Roger and the ABC leadership on the one hand, and key figures in Trafford Metropolitan Borough Council on the other, provide ABC with a good basis for seeking council help in any community-focused projects they may run.

Another area showing potential for further development is the possibility of establishing links between businesses in Trafford and Jinja. Many Christian leaders in Jinja are involved in regenerating that town and may have experience and expertise that could help people in the deprived parts of Trafford. The council's Chief Executive is keen to promote such exchanges of learning and ideas.

One other potential area for linking is between schools in the two communities. A school in Trafford that is bidding to become a science school is planning to set up links with a Jinja school. It is hoped that others may follow.

Roger discovered that a large number of UK local authorities have twinning links with local authorities in the Two Thirds World, and the Local Government International Bureau promotes such links and can supply a list of those that exist to date. Roger notes: 'The Trafford-Jinja link is becoming a good example . . . In the light of our experience, I would encourage churches to consider establishing links with churches in countries with which their council might already have such a link, or to help create one if none exist at present. Churches often represent sizeable community groups, and are in a position to help breathe life into a twinning or friendship arrangement.'

Impact of Ugandan visits on members of ABC and its local community

After the visit in February 2003, over fifty members of ABC had been to Uganda. Two of them, Christine Booth and Mike Wright, speak movingly of the impact that these visits have had on them and other church members: 'The changes in us and all those who have visited have probably been the biggest outcome so far of the whole enterprise. Contact with so many Ugandans who have few material goods and so many problems, but who are happy, contented and dignified, have forced us and others to rethink our own attitudes and goals and reassess those of our society. "Simplicity" has become a key word. We have realised how complicated our western lifestyle is, and how much we devote to protecting what we have, when what really matters is relationship. We found the whole experience profoundly liberating.'

Another spin-off was that returning ABC members inevitably talked about their experiences to non-Christian friends and colleagues, which could lead to interesting conversations about faith. The whole involvement by ABC in a poor community in Africa has added to its credibility in the local community. The programme to sponsor children at the Nile Vocational Institute, which is open to Trafford residents and anyone with the heart to help, as well as ABC members, gives a point of contact between the church and local residents.

Advice to others contemplating church-to-church partnerships

'Relationships are everything', says Roger. The whole thing has been a journey along which we have had to learn who we could trust, and to whom we should give money. Take as much advice as you can from people who know – but inevitably you won't be able to take in and act on everything you are told. A lot of prayer is needed. Don't commit early. Be prepared to make mistakes. The whole business is complex and messy, it will cost you a lot and you will get hurt.' Christine and Mike add: 'Take it slowly, proceed with gentle caution. Try and tune into the local culture and be open to thinking outside our western mindset. Partnership should be born out of a relationship and not be an end in itself.'

Further information on UgandAid can be obtained from ugandaid@aol.com.

If you would like to explore the possibility of setting up a church-to-church partnership in the context of town twinning arrangements, the Local Government International Bureau can supply details of town twinning links that already exist in your area. You can contact them at:

LGIB
Local Government House
London SW1P 3HZ
Tel: 020 7664 3100
Email: enquiries@lgib.gov.uk

8

Rugeley Community Church

GLOBAL LINKS: *Brazil*

CONGREGATION SIZE (2003): *around 65 adults*

CHURCH GROUPING: *Independent, linked to New Frontiers International*

Rugeley is a medium-sized town in Staffordshire, north of Birmingham, in what was once a coal-mining area. The two local mines closed some years ago, and only one of the two power stations now remains open. Unemployment is therefore high, and the jobs that are available in the immediate area are usually quite poorly paid. It is a place that seldom hits the headlines and which lives largely in the shadow of its neighbours, Stafford, Lichfield and Birmingham.

Rugeley Community Church is situated on a housing estate one mile from the centre of town. It is a charismatic church linked to the New Frontiers International movement with around sixty-five adult members plus children and teens. Its congregation (being a fair cross-section of the local community) is not wealthy; in 2002 the church's total budget was less than £40,000, from which the pastor's salary and building costs as well as all other expenses had to be paid.

In 1998 the pastor Nigel Lloyd heard a taped talk by Marcos Barros on the subject of covenant. At the time Nigel had no idea who Marcos Barros was, but he was so struck by what Marcos said about relationship and partnership that he resolved to track him down. This took several weeks, but eventually he discovered that Marcos was a Brazilian pastor from the missionary movement Go to the Nations (GTTN), who was now living in England. Nigel invited Marcos to preach at the Rugeley church in 1999, and for a year or two thereafter, captured by the vision of GTTN, Nigel attended some of their gatherings and invited occasional Brazilians visiting the UK to speak at his church.

At the same time David and Marjorie Judd moved from Kent to Rugeley and joined the church. David and Marjorie had been missionaries in Brazil in the 1970s and had a heart for the nations and particularly Brazil. They could sense that God seemed to be bringing something together but they didn't know how it would develop.

In this period the Rugeley congregation as a whole, though welcoming to any visitors, did not have enough direct contact with the Brazilians to buy into the vision, and it was seen as a personal enthusiasm of Nigel's. As he says: 'It is difficult to "get" what Go to the Nations is all about until you have experienced it.' However all this changed when, early in 2001, Nigel was asked by GTTN if his church would host a group of 35 young people from a church in the Brazilian city of Goiania in June that year. Nigel put the idea to the church and was simply amazed by their reaction. His wife Cally said: 'It felt as if God had done a work in the hearts of people even before the Brazilians came. Many people offered to put them up, including some people who had never before had visitors to stay.'

The visitors from Goiania

People from the church adopted the young people into their families as if they were their own. Charles and Wendy Adams with their children Joe (then eleven) and Emily (then eight) offered to host two of the young visitors, even though they felt apprehensive about taking into their home two strangers who spoke little or no English. They need not have worried. 'Within hours of their arrival God started to change us,' they say. 'We connected at heart level. Language was occasionally a problem but we usually got over it quite easily.' The children loved their visitors. Another couple, Scott and Gemma Mason, also hosted two of the Brazilian visitors, and were astounded at how their life was 'turned upside down in just a few days.'

The young Brazilians also had a considerable impact on the wider community. A secondary school in the town gave up a day of teaching so that the team could do drama and dance during lesson time. They also performed in the town centre, gathering large crowds, and being surprised by local shopkeepers who came out to thank them for their good behaviour! One night there was a walk to Cannock Chase, a local beauty spot, and a town councillor rang to see if he could come along and bring his family. Back at Rugeley Community Church, the visit helped to kickstart a youth group.

Nigel says that 'God did something in the hearts of both communities which is hard to explain, drawing us together in mutual love and support and transcending the language and cultural barriers. After they left, we felt like we'd lost a limb.'

The return visits to Goiania

The pastor of the Goiania church, Andre Calcada, invited Nigel to take a team from Rugeley to visit them in Brazil. The first group of seven went later that same year. In 2002 teams again visited in both directions, each team staying with members of the other church and joining in their life and activities. Thirteen out of what were then 65 members of the Rugeley church went to Brazil over the two visits.

Those who went from Rugeley were of all ages and included the Adams family and the Masons. 'Those who went in the main were not the ones you'd have expected to go,' said Nigel. Some had never been abroad before. Apart from Nigel (whose fare was paid by the church), everyone who went funded themselves. This was far from easy for those on low incomes, and the personal sacrifice involved in raising their air fares is a reflection of the priority they attached to making the visit and the love that had grown between them and their Brazilian friends.

Charles Adams is clear that their visit in 2002 changed the whole outlook of his family. 'We now see that church can be local and international as well, and realise it's not enough to restore God's people at home – we've got to go to the nations as well (see Isaiah 49:6).' Joe Adams says simply: 'The Brazilians make me feel happy and closer to God.' Charles described visiting a home for street girls as one of the most moving experiences of the visit. 'It was run by two young couples on next to nothing, but with so much love and joy. Not only were they making real personal sacrifices, but they were doing unglamorous long-term work. The girls were not just rescued and rehabilitated, but taught to evangelise others.'

Gemma Mason said: 'It was an amazing experience – something we never dreamed we'd do. But we really wanted to see what God was doing in Brazil.' Scott added:

'The joy on the Brazilians' faces when we arrived was almost embarrassing. They were so happy and pleased we were there. Their faith is so simple and Bible-based. I had wondered how deep it really went, but they were the same every day. Whenever I was with them, I felt you could reach out and touch God. While there you found yourself doing things you'd never dream of doing over here – and enjoying it.' They don't stop worshipping God when church is finished. Everywhere they go, God goes with them. And wherever they are they want to talk about Jesus. There is a continuing deep love between us, based on God.' Gemma recalls how at the farewell party before they left Goiania 'everyone was in tears.'

Ongoing links and longer term aims

The personal relationships built between members of the churches are maintained between visits by email, letters and phone calls. Although the Brazilians can be erratic correspondents, 'their letters are always full of the Lord.' One young Brazilian man has become such a close friend of the Adams family that he sends regular emails with news, requests for advice, and prayer requests, and asks them to send the family's prayer needs back so that he can pray for them. Both sides long for more visits.

The long-term aim is to work together in mission in a third country. The Brazilians want to send a team to the Athens Olympics in 2004 via Rugeley, which they would like to use as a training base. There is also talk of sending someone from either church to spend several months in the other country.

It has not all been plain sailing. Early in 2002 Pastor Andre's wife Liliane, who was in her thirties, suffered a massive stroke which has left her semi-paralysed down one side. The two churches prayed fervently for her but it meant that a visit to the UK had to be cancelled. Another issue is that economic difficulties in Brazil make it increasingly difficult for Brazilians to find the money to pay for visits to Britain.

Impact of the link on Rugeley Community Church

Nigel is realistic in recognising that the Brazilians are still human and fallible. He was saddened to see that when differences arose among leaders of a Brazilian church about the direction the church should take, there was a tendency for the church leaders and membership to split. This usually resulted in a new church being established, whereas a more mature approach might have been for the leaders to work through their differences and hold the church together. This was the sort of issue where the experience of British churches probably had something to offer them.

Nigel's wife Cally comments: 'Just as Israel in Old Testament times had a rich spiritual heritage which it could draw on even when its national and spiritual life was at a low ebb, so the church in Britain also has a rich Christian heritage and history. Despite the secularism and lack of passion in many of our churches today, that heritage is something of real value which we can offer to the new life, passion and enthusiasm of the Brazilian revival. We need each other and complement each other.'

The impact of the Brazilian connection has however been deep and lasting in Rugeley Community Church. Describing how the church has changed since the first group from Goiania visited in summer 2001, Nigel says: 'It had been a very introspective church, but it's now become global in outlook. Our members feel closer to the congregation in Goiania than to some churches in our own area. They regularly pray both for the church in Goainia and for a church in South Africa with which we have made a link. Relationships within the church have greatly improved. The Brazilians' love for God made us feel we loved God more. It brought people in the church closer together. Our prayer meetings are more global, and the style of our services has been affected by the Brazilian message of relationship. Putting people within another culture to share the lives of their hosts was in itself a life-changing experience for the majority of those who have been to Goiania.'

9

Emmanuel Church, South Croydon

GLOBAL LINKS: *The Ukraine and others*

CONGREGATION SIZE (2003): *around 450*

DENOMINATION: *Anglican*

Emmanuel Church is a flourishing evangelical church in the suburban setting of South Croydon, Surrey. Many members are middle-class professionals.

World mission has long been a significant part of Emmanuel's life, and since its foundation in 1899 many have been 'sent out' from the church to serve in full-time mission in other countries. By the mid-1980s, however, the church leadership was troubled by the declining numbers of those from the congregation volunteering for mission service, and aware that the general climate for mission was changing, without being clear how they should respond.

A deliberate strategy for mission

They therefore undertook a complete reappraisal of their own approach to mission, and the strategy which emerged had several strands

● Supporting Christians within their own countries and cultures
● All mission links are based on personal relationships. Emmanuel will only support a mission agency if there is someone within the congregation who will champion that link
● Aiming at a broad spread, both geographically and in types of mission
● Encouraging and recognising the value of short-term missionary service and visits (which had previously rather been frowned upon as 'not a proper commitment')
● The church makes no distinction, so far as its own organisation is concerned, between mission in the UK outside the local area and mission in other countries. Both come under a Mission Committee.

Rob Burch, a member of the Mission Committee, explains some other policies that have been adopted by the church: 'For some time we have had a rule that no representative of a mission agency will be invited to preach unless their preaching has been heard before and they are considered to be good. A bad missionary preacher can do immense damage and resurrect some of the unfortunate stereotyping of missionaries which figured in the past!'

'The church only supports people in long-term mission from the UK if pension provision forms part of their practical support arrangements from the start. This rule was adopted as a result of our experience with some missionaries whom we had supported long-term, but who returned to the UK on retirement with virtually no pension or other means of support. We managed to raise funds to help provide them with some security, but are now determined to ensure that such a situation does not arise again.'

At one point, Emmanuel also sought to begin a church-to-church partnership with a church in Zimbabwe. The minister had been studying and living in Croydon for a year and become well known in the church, so when he was about to return to Zimbabwe, Emmanuel Church suggested setting up a partnership with his church. However the parishes proved to be too dissimilar. While Emmanuel was wealthy and suburban, the Zimbabwean parish was poor, rural, and covered an area as big as a whole English diocese. The relationship became one-sided and unequal, with Emmanuel sending money for church projects and the Zimbabwean parish only able to send a few visitors to the UK. Neighbouring churches in Zimbabwe became resentful at the money this one church was receiving, and the local Bishop in Zimbabwe also expressed objections to the relationship. In the face of these difficulties, the relationship was ended. As a result of this experience Emmanuel concluded that attempting to form church-to-church partnerships with Anglican churches in the Two-Thirds World was tricky.

Support for Christians working in mission within their own cultures

As a result of their strategy review in the mid-1980s, Emmanuel took the view that mission undertaken by people working within their own culture is a more efficient and effective form than mission undertaken cross-culturally. The practical outworking of this is that for mission work in other countries their main aim is to adopt a partnering or supporting role. There are a number of examples of this

1. Ukraine. Emmanuel now meets the salary costs of the pastor of a group of Baptist churches and a youth worker. Before Emmanuel committed to supporting this work, their vicar went to meet the Ukrainian pastor and youth worker in order to get to know them both and satisfy himself and the church that they were people whom they could trust. Through this link teams of young people are sent from Emmanuel to help at Ukrainian summer camps under local leadership. Personal relationships are maintained between the Ukrainians and members of Emmanuel through regular visits from Emmanuel including the summer teams, and visits to Croydon by the Ukranian leadership team – many friendships are being built. Emmanuel's funding for the two Ukrainians is mediated through a third party, Scripture Union International, which helped to set up and continues to support the relationship. This helps to minimise the imbalance that the money element could have created in the relationship. In fact the relationship seems genuinely two-way, with both sides gaining spiritually. For example, members of the Emmanuel team visiting the Ukraine each summer always return saying they learnt an enormous amount from the experience.

2. Uganda. Emmanuel supports four Ugandan students who are in theological training in Uganda. The church would generally be reluctant to support students who come to the UK to study unless there are no suitable study/training centres in their own or nearby countries. This is because the cost of supporting someone to live and study in the UK is usually much higher than such costs would be nearer their own homes. Furthermore, those who come to the west from southern countries can often become so used to the comforts and other material advantages that they become reluctant to return to live in their own countries.

3. India. The church supports an Indian couple undertaking pastoral work amongst the Indian community in the Middle East.
4. Tajikistan. Support is also given to local church leaders in Tajikistan engaged in outreach work among young people.

Supporting Emmanuel Church members in mission

Despite their emphasis on supporting indigenous workers in mission, Emmanuel also supports established members of its own congregation who feel called to go to other countries. First though, such individuals will normally be assessed by the vicar and the Mission Committee, and if there is consensus that God is indeed calling them to this work, the church will commit to supporting them financially and in prayer and, if they are going out long-term, pastorally. Church members young and mature also go on short-term mission teams or to help with projects in other countries with the church's support.

In 2003 two members of Emmanuel Church were working overseas on a longer term basis, one in Zimbabwe with the Oasis Trust and another based in Kenya undertaking literacy and church support in the Sudan. Contact with these church members is maintained by means of visits from the church as well as letters, email and telephone contacts.

Visits to mission partners – a key part of the mission strategy

Visits by Emmanuel leaders and members to people and projects with which they have a link are central to their mission strategy and help to keep mission at the forefront of the church life. In 2002 groups and individuals from the church undertook visits to the Ukraine, Kenya, Brazil and Zimbabwe with about fifteen church members in all going on these trips. Rob Burch puts it this way: 'If we can get large numbers of church members experiencing missionary work at the coal-face, or at least having close friends doing it, the rest of the missionary support activities will almost run themselves!'

Ensuring that their leaders share the vision for mission has been given priority; Rob says 'Sending successive clergy on overseas visits has, perhaps, been our best investment. They have all captured the vision in a new way which has not only benefited us but, I am sure, the churches to which they moved on to.' Adrian Youings, senior curate at Emmanuel, describes how his first overseas visit from the church affected him: 'The impact on me was enormous. Making such a personal link with individuals involved in overseas mission gave me a passion for supporting mission which hadn't really been there before. It's helped me to encourage others to take a real interest in mission too. I took a team of five others back to the same place the following year.'

Those wanting to go on a visit need to be approved by the vicar and Mission Committee. The church is so convinced of the value of such trips that it is ready to fund the costs of the prospective visitors, though in practice many people pay their own way.

The church publicises visits in advance and arranges feedback sessions on return, which are well attended from across the congregation. Visits have a huge impact on those who go and have led to several considering whether God is calling them to longer term service in mission.

The visits are also highly valued by those who are visited, who have said they thought money was well spent because of the encouragement and sense of renewed support that they received.

Funding mission work

Every year the church holds an Annual Pledge Day at which church members pledge an amount to church funds and a separate amount to the Mission Fund. In 2002 Mission Fund income was £48,000 and the church's General Fund income was £283,000. Occasionally gifts are also received separately, but Emmanuel has no regular collections for mission except on Christmas Day, when the money is sent to a local charity.

Integration of global mission into the life of the church

As well as the central role played by pastoral and fact-finding visits overseas by church leaders and members, mission is integrated in church life by several other means: Live interviews with those who go on visits, ensuring that missionaries are featured in church prayers every week on a rota basis, and occasional special events, are all elements in the strategy. The use of a telephone line permanently connected to the church PA system enables good quality two-way phone conversations with missionaries and church members overseas during services. This has brought immediacy to missionary work. 'For example,' says Rob, 'we may have an interview and prayer for someone just about to go overseas one Sunday, and then have them interviewed by phone telling us their first impressions the following Sunday.

'As a result of Emmanuel's purposeful approach to mission, instead of traditional missionary spots in services led by enthusiastic supporters, and a small loyal band of people who attend special missionary meetings, there is far more of a sense of integration of overseas mission into

many aspects of the life of the church. Despite all that we
are doing in mission we feel that there is room for so much
more – we are never satisfied!'

10

Oldmachar Church, Aberdeen

GLOBAL LINKS: *The Ukraine*

CONGREGATION SIZE (2003): *about 220*

DENOMINATION: *Church of Scotland*

Bridge of Don is a suburb of the city of Aberdeen in Scotland that sprung up to provide housing mainly for those attracted to the city during the North Sea oil boom. Local residents are typically dual-income, middle-class professionals in an area where unemployment runs at only 2 per cent. Many of the residents stay for only a short time, spending just a few years in Aberdeen before they move on.

Oldmachar Church was planted in 1993 from a Church of Scotland church to serve the growing area of Bridge of Don. In the early years the Oldmachar congregation met in church halls but they later moved to a redundant church building. As a church plant the church has more freedom in style and worship than traditional churches within the Church of Scotland.

In 1998 Graham Black, the first minister of the church, and his wife Hazel received a mailing from Radstock Ministries containing an article about the political situation in the Ukraine. It mentioned that legislation was about to be implemented there which would curtail the freedom that churches had gained in 1990 after the fall of communism, and urged churches in the UK to befriend Ukrainian churches.

Graham recalls: 'Something about the situation of the church in the Ukraine touched our hearts and we decided to find out more. We also thought that linking with a church from a very different setting would help to widen the outlook of our congregation as we had no heritage of overseas mission involvement. People within the church had little real interest in traditional forms of mission support, such as praying and giving towards sending western missionaries to work in other countries.'

They therefore contacted Jill Kingston, Radstock's coordinator for Russia and the Ukraine. She visited them and put them in touch with a Ukrainian Pentecostal church of similar size to their own that had been planted in 1992. After initial contacts were made, Hazel and Graham started planning a visit to the Ukraine to obtain firsthand information about the Ukrainians' outlook, context and needs, and the prospects for building a partnership. Later in 1998 Hazel went alone with Jill and met the pastor, Slava Laguti, and his congregation. At the last moment Graham had to pull out of the trip due to a depressive illness, but it was through this very illness that the first blessing from the Ukrainian link came for him and his family.

'When we arrived, Slava asked why Graham had been unable to come,' recalls Hazel. 'I explained Graham's illness and Slava, his wife and other church leaders immediately said "let's pray for him". They promptly got down on their knees and prayed for Graham for some time.

When we had finished, Slava gave me some Bible references that he believed God had given him for Graham. One of these in particular provided a lifeline of hope that Graham was to cling to in the dark months of depression that still awaited him. It was Isaiah 45:3: "I will give you the treasures of darkness, riches stored in secret places, so that you may know that I am the LORD, the God of Israel, who summons you by name"' (New International Version).

The setting for the Ukrainian church that Hazel visited was far from glamorous – an out-of the-way town called Ternovka, where the only industry was coal mining. Life there was hard, and Pastor Slava's wife Natasha worked down a mine herself to earn money for the family to live on. None of the congregation had a professional background. The contrast with the church in Aberdeen could hardly have been greater.

During the visit, Hazel was grilled on theological issues by her hosts and some other church leaders whom she met. Infant baptism (which the Church of Scotland practises but Pentecostals do not!) was a controversial issue for them. However Slava and his church leaders had a broad outlook, and the welcome Hazel was given and the relationships she began to build with members of the Ukrainian church were enough to convince her, and the Oldmachar Church leadership on her return, that this link should be strengthened.

Because his depression lingered for some time, Graham felt obliged to give up church leadership in June 1999, although he remained a member of Oldmachar Church. 'It was a difficult and painful time for all of us,' he says. 'I was forced to reconsider all that I had taken for granted about myself and particularly my gifting for ministry. I felt as if I was being taken to pieces, but slowly as the months passed, I realised that the Lord was reshaping my life and opening up a very different type of ministry from the one for which I had previously felt equipped. This new ministry was essentially informal and pastoral, and the Ukraine was to play a very important role in it.'

In August 1999 Graham paid his first visit to the Ukraine, wanting to thank Slava, Natasha, and their church for the concern and support they had shown towards him when Hazel had visited, as well as to build up the relationship between the two churches. Until that visit Graham had had very little firsthand contact with charismatic congregations, and he confesses to feeling at first rather superior towards the emotionalism and hype which he associated with the Pentecostalism of his hosts. However, as he recounts: 'The experience of worshipping with them caused a profound change in my heart. I felt the beginning of a spiritual freedom that was right outside my previous experience and theological training. It was an awakening to the reality of the Holy Spirit.' This alone was enough to make the Ukraine special to him, but by the end of his visit he also had a sense that the Ukraine was very much on God's agenda for his own future.

In 2000 Jill Kingston asked Graham to work with her as part of Radstock in encouraging and supporting the churches in the Ukraine. It was from this time that Graham's new ministry began to take shape – pastoring of pastors, in the Ukraine as well as in Scotland. Later that year he went back to the Ukraine and visited again in 2001 and 2002. The programme for his visits was often unclear when he set out, but each time the building of relationships and giving pastoral encouragement to Pentecostal and Baptist pastors and other church leaders whom God put in his path, proved to be the crucial element for him. The church in the Ukraine had gone through a period of rapid growth during the nineties and seen the emergence of young and gifted leaders. But like rapidly growing churches elsewhere, these leaders often lacked mature and experienced Christians who could give them support and encouragement. Graham also did regular teaching and preaching, bringing a wider perspective and depth of theology that the churches there found helpful.

'On each trip I saw at firsthand the amazing work that God was doing in the lives of people who had no other hope. I saw congregations comprised largely of reformed alcoholics and drug addicts who had been empowered by the Holy Spirit to overcome their addictions. Churches and individuals were deeply involved in reaching out to the neediest people in their communities, and seeing dramatic conversions and healings. But I also saw the same manifestations of human sinfulness that afflict the church elsewhere – spiritual pride, selfishness, competitiveness, and disunity, to mention but a few – and the discouragement that they often caused to church leaders. I found that from my own experiences of brokenness and apparent failure, and by the grace of God, I was able to comfort and encourage those who were being pushed to their limits by the demands being made of them.

'It has been amazing to see how God has been able to use these contacts for his purposes, despite the very real language barrier. I have little understanding of Russian and my Ukrainian friends have no knowledge of English, so we are all very reliant on interpreters for effective communication. More than once there has been a crisis when interpreting arrangements have fallen through at the last moment but always some alternative has been found.'

Two-way benefits

Graham is in no doubt that he and his church have far more to gain from the church link than the Ukrainian Christians have. He has been deeply impressed by the Ukrainians' living faith. 'The whole of their life is faith. They have no one and nothing to depend on save God. Their freshness and vibrancy have encouraged us tremendously. We feel the impoverished ones. And their commitment to mission and evangelism, including practical social action, puts us to shame.' His reactions were shared by the new minister of Oldmachar Church and a church elder, who both accompanied Graham on his visit in 2000. On their return they said: 'What can we give to them? They have so much to give to us.' They witnessed real evidence of the power of God in the Ukrainians' worship and intercession. This experience has encouraged the Bridge of Don church to move into the gifts of the Spirit, in ways which have strengthened the church and its members and encouraged it into greater openness to God and each other.

Shortly after the fall of communism, the Ukrainian churches had experienced 'hit and run' missionaries from the USA and Scandinavia, who poured in resources for a few years but then withdrew from the fledgling churches they had encouraged into being. Graham discovered that Ukrainian churches – isolated from outside contacts for so many years under communism – valued the link with him and his church partly because it was tangible evidence of a continuing interest in them by the wider global church. In addition, they knew that they needed sound teaching and training in Christian living and were deeply appreciative of the input he was able to give. Graham also came to realise that they needed encouragement to simply be what they were in Christ and not to give in to the temptation to ape those who came from beyond Ukraine. 'God has set them in *their* country and culture, and it is for them to live prayerfully as the church in appropriate ways.'

One legacy of the involvement by American and Scandinavian Christians in the Ukraine was that it had left Ukrainian Christians mesmerised by western models of being church. As a result the Ukrainians often hanker after their own large church buildings, rather than being content to use rented property. Some churches seemed to want partnership with a western church mainly so that they could tap into funds to help them realise this ambition. While Graham and Hazel were entirely satisfied that Slava did not value a link with their church for what it could give his church materially, his church too had embarked on a church-building scheme. Despite some reservations about the wisdom of this course, Oldmachar Church has contributed to the project.

A growing relationship

Until early 2003, direct contacts with the Ukrainian Christians by those at Bridge of Don had been confined to Graham, Hazel, and the minister and elder who went out with Graham in 2000. So while the congregation as a whole enjoyed indirect benefits from their experiences and contributed generously to the Ukraine church's building programme, they had had no opportunity to be directly impacted by the Ukrainians' faith, worship and relationship with God. This changed however, when in March 2003, Slava and his wife paid their first visit to Aberdeen.

'This visit proved to be a wonderful experience,' says Graham. 'Perhaps the most significant thing was the sense of relationships being formed which will be deepened in the future. As Slava and Natasha met with people at Oldmachar, there was a true sense of God uniting the Church of Grace, Ternovka, with Oldmachar Church. Within the space of ten days, two couples had made plans to visit Ternovka. Deeper spiritual parallels were uncovered, and patterns of struggle, pain, blessing and growth became apparent. What God was doing in one place, he either had done or was doing in the other. This lifted the relationship far beyond a human one into the realms of God's activity and grace.

'The Ukrainians are keen to hold a teaching conference for church leaders in their area, and have invited me and others from Scotland to deliver teaching,' explains Graham. 'As always this requires deep sensitivity to God's Spirit, so that what we teach and the way we teach is not at all patronising, but is offered in grace and humility. "Foreigners" have made regrettable mistakes in this area due to lack of established relationships, but an opportunity now arises out of relationship which can be harnessed for the Kingdom.'

A miracle in Ukraine leads to another in Aberdeen

Graham tells a story that perhaps epitomises the way in which this developing relationship is bringing blessing to Christians in both countries.

'When I visited the Ukraine in 2000, I met an old Baptist pastor called Dmitriy Romanuk who told me something of his own life story. Dmitriy's father had been a pastor in the communist era. One night there was a knock at the door and he was arrested and taken to prison. His family never saw him again, but five years later learnt he had been shot. So when Dmitriy later obeyed a call from God to become a pastor he was under no illusions about the possible consequences. Some years after this, when the communists were still in control, Dmitriy had to go to hospital because of a high fever and infection. When the nurse discovered he was a pastor, she summoned the matron and senior nursing staff. They stood around his bed and said that if he did not renounce Jesus Christ, they would give him a lethal injection because he was an enemy of the State.

Dmitriy refused to renounce Jesus so a syringe filled with poison was brought. At this point in the story Dmitriy pulled up the cuffs of his suit and shirt and showed me his purple-veined wrist. "This is where she injected me," he said, placing his index finger on the pulse point. "As the needle went in I know it was not time to die so I cried out: 'Jesus save me!' The poison entered his bloodstream, but it had no effect on his body.

'I was deeply moved by this story and back in Scotland recounted it to a prayer group in which one member, Rebekah, had suffered for four years from a severe allergy to latex rubber. Everywhere she went she had to take an emergency supply of adrenaline. A touch of anything containing latex would cause her to go into anaphylactic shock which untreated could bring death within minutes. Even a sip from a cup washed by hands wearing rubber gloves would result in vastly swollen lips and cracked skin. Rebekah listened intently to Dmitriy's story, and at the end she burst into tears, which quickly gave way to near-hysteria. Eventually she managed to compose herself but no one knew what had happened.

'In fact God had spoken to her and challenged her complete trust in the adrenaline shot. As she confessed that and placed her trust in Jesus, as Dmitriy had done, so God began to set her free. Ten days later she decided to test this sense of freedom. She and her husband prayed and read the promises of God in Scripture. Then she unpacked a sterile latex glove, touched it and brushed her cheek with it. The only result was a very slight swelling of her lips and eyes. The following Sunday she put the glove on for half an hour. Nothing at all happened! Her health visitor broke down in tears when told the story. Her friends, several of them atheists, had been well aware of her condition because of the precautions they had had to take whenever she visited them. In order to tell them what had happened,

Rebekah invited them round one by one and welcomed them into a living room filled with balloons. While their jaws hit the floor she testified to what the living God had done in her life. Her GP referred her to an allergy unit for complete testing. There the highly sceptical medical consultant tested her with the strongest possible solution of latex, but obtained no reaction; none of the antibodies associated with her allergy were found in her blood. In profound puzzlement he said: 'This looks like a miracle.' Only when the full range of tests had been concluded did Rebekah give her full testimony, concluding: 'What you see is the effect of the power of the resurrected Son of God, Jesus Christ. He has healed me!'

11

Christ Church, Fulwood (Sheffield)

GLOBAL LINKS: *Romania and the Ukraine*

CONGREGATION SIZE (2003): *850-1,000*

DENOMINATION: *Anglican*

Christ Church, Fulwood is situated in a residential suburb
of Sheffield. Membership is around eight hundred and fifty,
but adult attendance at the three Sunday services is about a
thousand. Many of those who come live well outside the
parish boundaries, and it is a popular church with students.

The church has a long tradition of mission support,
most of it focused on individuals who have gone into
mission work from the church. Roughly 20 per cent of the
church's income goes to overseas mission, and in 2001 this
amounted to some £115,000. Support from Christ Church
for mission work in the UK and overseas is overseen by
the Missionary Committee. Broadly speaking, the church
supports work that its members feel called to, provided
that the call has first been tested and agreed by the vicar
and church council. Those supported serve with a wide
range of agencies and projects around the world. In 2002,

23 individuals or couples working through a number of agencies were being supported in mission by the church. Additionally the church supports several mission agencies and some specific projects.

Christ Church also has two partnerships with churches in the former Soviet Bloc, each of which has been going for over ten years. One is in Romania, the other in the Eastern Ukraine. Each link is run by a separate committee composed of people with a strong commitment to the relationship.

The Romania link

As Romania opened up to the west after the fall of the communist regime, the sad state of its economy and people became widely known and people at Christ Church wanted to help. A former member of the church's staff, Dave Fenton, contacted the mission agency Eurovangelism, which had been supporting churches in Eastern Europe for some years, and was put in touch with a Romanian Baptist pastor and his church. The initial aim was to encourage and strengthen the local church and its evangelistic efforts, but once direct contacts were established this aim soon broadened.

The first party from Christ Church went out in 1991 taking relief supplies to the church, and there has since been a relief aid trip every autumn along with other visits by individuals and groups. Substantial amounts of money were raised towards a new church building for the Romanians along with materials needed for the building, and during trips, members of Christ Church also contributed specific skills as well as labour towards the construction. The church was opened in 1997.

Christ Church has however gone much further than just supplying relief and contributing to the church building

and particularly tried to give general encouragement and
support to the Romanian Christians and to build up
personal relationships. Soon after direct contacts were
made with the first church, links were also established
with several other village churches. Personal relationships
between individuals in both countries have been
important in keeping the church links going, and some
church members give financial assistance to some of the
Christians they know well.

Money and goods have in fact been a significant element
in this relationship. In addition to the aid already
mentioned, Christ Church has given regularly to support
the pastors of some of the churches, and contributed to the
running costs of the church buildings. As time has passed,
however, they have become increasingly aware of the
dangers of heavy financial involvement. Dave Ling, a
member of the Romania Committee, comments: 'Possibly
our relationship has been based too much on the material
and not sufficiently on the spiritual. Our response to
poverty and deprivation is naturally to pour money in –
and raising money does conveniently involve our whole
congregation in the link on a practical level. But we have
probably not been quick enough to shift the emphasis on
to the spiritual. We want to make the Romanian side
understand more fully that it is a two-way link, and that
they have much to offer us. Our support for the pastors
needs to be kept under careful review. The level of support
can easily be wrong, and dependence could become a
stumbling block. We have to know when and where it
might be wiser to limit support – so we need to be in close
touch with what is going on in the church in order to avoid
funding things which are not in keeping with our
principles. We also need to avoid appearing to dictate just
because we hold some purse strings. The emphasis of our
support is therefore now moving away from finance and

goods and towards relationships and spiritual cooperation.'

From the late nineties a significant problem emerged with this relationship. Dave Ling remembers how the Romania Committee at Christ Church became increasingly concerned about the pastor of the main Romanian church: 'We felt he was authoritarian and used inappropriate discipline with his church members. He tried to limit and control direct communications by those members with Christ Church, apparently so that he could be the sole conduit for all contacts. We felt that he had gerrymandered his church committee to exclude those who questioned or opposed him, and we became increasingly suspicious that he might have misappropriated some of the gifts that we had sent. In 2001 we finally decided that we could no longer support the pastor or his church committee, but would continue to take relief supplies to church members and maintain friendships with other individuals. Shortly after coming to this hard decision, the Romanian Baptist hierarchy removed the pastor, withdrew his authorisation to operate as a pastor within the Baptist church, and installed an interim replacement.'

Although this was obviously a difficult time in the relationship, Dave Ling says: 'We never seriously considered ending the link because of the strength of the personal friendships that had been built between members of both congregations. We have been hurt by all this, but less hurt than the partner church concerned, and we see our ongoing support for them as important in their rebuilding of the church there. In a sense, the adversity itself can be an element in strengthening our partnership. We have had to make hard decisions, but not as hard as those they have had to make. But now we're looking to the future. We have a good relationship with the interim pastor, an impressive student pastor who has been helping in the church has been appointed to become its assistant pastor from September 2003, and we are happy with the direction the church is taking now. A group of our young people went out to the area in the summer of 2002, to help with a children's camp – a successful venture which everyone involved hopes to repeat. In addition, in March 2003 our vicar visited the churches of the area to encourage and teach both pastors and people, and to demonstrate our wish to continue the partnership, but with more emphasis on the spiritual side. Plans are being made to take the partnership forward (including spiritual training, and linking families), and overall the relationship is emerging stronger than ever.'

For some years there was no written or agreed set of aims but when the difficulties with the Romanian pastor arose, the Christ Church Romania Committee felt they needed to be clearer on what they were about. A statement of aims has now been produced as a guide for the Committee. Though not formally agreed with the Romanians, these aims are the result of experience in contact with them, and are in keeping with their own expressed aims and desires. The stated aims are

● To encourage both churches and their members
● To provide support to the Romanians – materially, in prayer and by visiting
● To agree the basis of ministry with the Romanians
● Setting timescales for particular projects or objectives
● Supporting church and gospel activities, for example in youth and children's work
● Ensuring that contact is regularly maintained – by email, letters, phone calls, visits.

The Ukraine link

Not content with one partnership in Eastern Europe, Christ Church sought another. In the early 1990s Sheffield was twinned with the city of Donetsk in the Ukraine, and they thought a link with a church in that city would be a good place to start. They made inquiries through Radstock Ministries, which specialises in setting up church partnerships (see other stories in this book), and in 1992 were put in touch with the pastor of a Pentecostal church.

From the outset this partnership took a rather different course from the Romanian link. The aim was to assist the Ukrainians in evangelism in hospitals, orphanages, streets and parks; and also to train some of Christ Church's members in evangelism helping to encourage enthusiasm for mission among their own church members.

Over the years the aims have evolved, but money has played little part in them. In more than ten years Christ Church has only funded treatment for one disabled child, given a little money towards a building project, and provided help with visits to the UK for Ukrainians who would otherwise not have been able to go. There is an annual visit from Christ Church each summer, and sometimes a visit from Donetsk to the UK as well. Contact between visits is maintained mainly by email, though language can be a problem.

In recent years the Christ Church teams have helped with the Ukrainian church's annual summer camp. Here they have aimed to encourage the work, especially among teenagers, and to help with Bible study and music and drama. But training members of Christ Church in mission continues to be a significant aim. When such visits are taking place, prayer schemes are organised to involve all of Christ Church in prayer support.

Johnny Lockwood, who leads the Ukraine Committee, comments: 'The aims of the link change and develop over time as a need is identified, the situation changes, or as the talents of those involved differ from year to year. The relationship has remained healthy and popular because the Ukrainian pastor is innovative and introduces new elements to our activities from one year to the next. Each year the team that goes consists mainly of people new to the link. From our very first visit to the Ukraine, God told certain people to come. As I have learnt that he does this, I now advertise each visit in quite a low-key way.'

Partnering across denominations

Denominational issues have not proved a significant problem in either relationship. Johnny says of the Ukrainian link: 'Linking with a non-Anglican church has actually been helpful, as it has encouraged our people not to "assume" things about the other church – whether on doctrine, church services, or anything else. Their pastor loves to delve into his Bible and come up with questions and arguments late at night! I believe that he (and by implication the church) acknowledges our similarities and accepts our differences, although he was once a bit shocked by the deliberately ambiguous language of parts of the Anglican Communion service. They recognise that we have a less authoritarian view of how church members should live and act, despite our more hierarchical church structure. In matters of doctrine there are no significant divisions.'

Dave Ling comments on the Romanian church: 'Denominational issues may have been a bit of an issue on their side, but not sufficiently to cause problems in our normal contacts – no problems over taking communion, for example. They may have suspicions about us as Anglicans, but they have less of a tradition of blurring the edges, and they are coming to realise that we are not all like that. They have more of a tradition of discipline in the church which we sometimes find difficult, and in which we can see dangers. Issues such as infant baptism and confirmation have not really arisen as practical problems in our relationship.'

Support for the links

The Romania link has the higher profile within Christ Church, mainly because the yearly relief aid trip involves a wide number of people in giving and collecting goods. However when visitors have come to Sheffield from Donetsk and taken part in church activities this has highlighted the Ukrainian link to the congregation at large. Regular prayer updates are sent to the people directly involved and passed on to the congregation.

Dave is clear that for a church partnership to succeed 'it is vital to have support from the top. In a church the size of ours, where so much is happening all the time, it is difficult for the vicar to actively involve himself in everything we do; but his prayerful moral support, advice and guidance is an essential element. Our links are run by groups who are fully committed to them, but it is important that the vicar is kept well informed of what is happening so that he can get involved when appropriate.'

Advice to other churches considering a church-to-church partnership

Dave says: 'First, consider prayerfully and, if led by the Lord, go for it! Size and resources (spiritual, human and financial) of the church may affect the nature of the link, but I believe even a small, materially resourceless British church can have something to offer.

'Identify a target area, and get information and advice from Christian people or agencies who know it, its people, needs, culture and so on. It can be helpful if they direct you to an individual church/pastor with a particular need or project which your wider congregation can focus on and participate in, to get the link started.

'Look on it as a long-term project. We are dealing with our Christian brothers and sisters, and you don't just drop family after a few months or even years. It helps if the church leadership and a significant percentage of the members are committed to the link.

'Individual relationships strengthen the link, so try to go for somewhere that it is practical to visit from time to time, or where there is not an insurmountable language barrier.'

Benefits of partnering

Dave believes British Christians can learn from Romanian ones about fervency in prayer, sacrificial service for the Lord, loyalty to his church, how to live by faith rather than relying on our wealth/possessions, and learning better to respond to the Lord's prompting to act and give. He also thinks the Romanians could gain from us an interest in the church worldwide, and an understanding that 'seeking guidance from God's word and depending on God's grace are more important than following rules.'

Johnny says of the Ukrainian link: 'We can learn from them a deeper faith in the Lord to act and answer prayer, and acceptance of what he sends us. The Ukrainians could learn the value of systematic Bible study, and the importance of keeping children and young people in touch with the Lord and interested in his work.'

Summing up, Dave says: 'The more closely individuals involve themselves in these partnerships, the more they gain from them. In all cases I believe those here who have worked for the links would say it has been a positive experience in their Christian walk, and they have gained much by seeing how Christians in totally different circumstances put their faith into practice. However it is a messy business, simply because it involves sinners, and we have been hurt as well. All that said, I believe the pluses far outweigh the minuses, and would give positive encouragement to any church that felt led to partner with another in an unfamiliar culture. But you have to be ready to take the rough with the smooth.'

12

St Saviour's, Guildford

GLOBAL LINKS: *Various*

CONGREGATION SIZE (2003): *around 1,000*

DENOMINATION: *Anglican*

St Saviour's is a large evangelical Anglican church situated close to Guildford city centre, with an affluent, and predominantly professional, congregation. On a typical Sunday around six hundred and fifty people attend its services, with regular worshippers numbering around a thousand in all. St Saviour's has a long tradition of supporting mission work, and a steady stream of people goes out from the church on long, medium or short-term mission ventures. For a number of years Garth Hewitt, the singer-songwriter and campaigner for social justice, and his foundation the Amos Trust were based at St Saviour's, helping to ensure that social justice was seen to be at the heart of mission.

Becoming a 'mission community'

In recent years St Saviour's has had a growing sense that the privileges which it enjoys – in terms of material benefits, gifted members, and comfortable, attractive and versatile church buildings – are gifts from God to be given away. It has developed a commitment to becoming a 'mission community' as an expression of a church 'devoted to God, to each other, and to a broken world'. The church is in the process of discovering all that this commitment means, but at least two elements have already become clear. One is the need to encourage people into incorporating mission and an evangelistic outlook into the whole of their life. Another is the need to encourage, nurture and train a sense of Christian vocation in individuals, and then release them to participate in what God is doing in the world.

Against this background, St Saviour's takes the view that mission starts on their doorstep and ends at the furthermost parts of the earth. Since April 2002 they have had a Mission Pastor, Andrew Wheeler, who has oversight of all the church's mission activities from Alpha courses to the allocation of the mission budget: so there's no division of mission activities between 'home' and 'overseas' here! Andrew's post is a new one in the church, and he came to it after 23 years as a missionary with CMS in East Africa. He remains a CMS mission partner while at St Saviour's and his post is co-funded by CMS and St Saviour's. He also has a mission role within the Diocese of Guildford.

A mission training programme

One demonstration of St Saviour's commitment to mission is 'Get Connected', a full-time year-long discipleship and mission training programme which the church runs for people able to take a year out. Participants are drawn from its own and neighbouring congregations. In its first year, 2001-02, the course had eight members who were all taking a gap year between school and university. In the second year the numbers nearly doubled to 15, including some older people (in their thirties). It is hoped that this growth in numbers and the range of participants will grow in future years.

The course is run over three terms and includes two days each week of teaching on issues such as the Bible, mission and spiritual growth. Participants are also given placements in outreach programmes in Guildford, usually with young people, which occupy them for about ten hours each week. In addition, most participants undertake a weekly half-day programme, accredited by the University of Wales, in the principles and practice of working in voluntary organisations. Some course members work part-time to support themselves while on the programme. In the third term each student goes on an international placement of six to eight weeks which may be taken with a variety of mission bodies.

The success of this programme has led to a broader vision to make the training and other resources it offers available for the wider congregation of St Saviour's and neighbouring churches. From early 2003 courses are being offered on church premises covering a range of subjects, from Ignatian prayer to studies of Amos and issues of justice.

Role of the Mission Committee

St Saviour's has a strong and active Mission Committee with a passion for spreading the gospel and a willingness to wrestle with difficult issues. In recent years it has given serious thought to its role which it now sees as four-fold

- As a 'think tank' to work out what mission means for St Saviour's as a whole. One aspect of this is that they have developed a growing conviction that their church council is really the Mission Committee of the church
- Educational – to educate the whole congregation in mission and what it means for them
- To give personal and pastoral support to those from the congregation who are serving in mission
- Financial – raising and administering funds for mission purposes.

Giving to mission through strategic alliances

The church's mission budget is around £100,000 annually. Like many churches, it had in the past divided its mission funds multiple ways, often to satisfy those in the congregation wanting to see their favourite causes supported. Recently however the giving has become focused on what they call 'strategic alliances' with agencies or individuals with which they want to build reciprocal relationships locally, nationally and internationally. At a local level these strategic alliances include the YMCA, a network of local youth workers called Matrix, and Guildford for God, a movement which employs schools workers and family workers.

Internationally St Saviour's give priority to supporting their own members working in mission, but they have other links through which they aim not only to give but also to receive and learn. For example, they have close links with a Scripture Union worker in South Africa and with the Anglican Church in Egypt, especially a bishop there. They gave a proportion of the money raised for refurbishing St Saviour's church premises to help rebuild a church in

Egypt. There have been visits both ways to South Africa and Egypt, often funded by St Saviour's. Teams of young people from Guildford have been to South Africa on short-term mission trips arranged through their linked Scripture Union worker. The Anglican bishop from Egypt had a huge impact on the congregation at St Saviour's when he spent some time visiting them in 2002, as much by the quality of his life and evident faith as by what he said.

Many young people at St Saviour's are members of Crusaders, the national youth movement, and have taken part in camps and visits to Romania organised in conjunction with Cristia, a Romanian youth organisation. This has led to close ties with Cristia, and St Saviour's shared in the visit of three Cristia members to Guildford. Such links enable the congregation at St Saviour's to broaden their outlook and understanding, and get some very different perspectives on faith, life and mission. The church also retains strong links with the Amos Trust, CMS and other agencies and many of its young people go on gap year placements every year with organisations which include the Oasis Trust, YWAM, Latin Link and Soapbox.

Not a mission agency!

Because it is such a large and wealthy church, it would be possible for St Saviour's to become a quasi-mission agency itself, sending and supporting its own people. But it has always resisted this temptation, believing that its members would generally be better served by linking with mission agencies which know about sending and supporting people in mission, and which have other relevant experience and expertise.

St Saviour's and Anglican Companion Links

As described in the chapter on The Lyndhurst Deanery and Rwanda, every diocese in England has links with other parts of the Anglican Communion around the world. Historically St Saviour's has not participated in Guildford Diocese's Companion Links which are principally with the Anglican Church in Nigeria. This lack of participation in Companion Links seems to be a common theme for evangelical Anglican churches around the UK. This could be a missed opportunity, especially as the Anglican Church in many places overseas is often strongly evangelical. 'I hope that at St Saviour's our involvement in Companion Links will change and that relationships will grow with the church in Nigeria,' comments Andrew Wheeler. 'The Companion Links enable an important level of cross-cultural learning to take place. Those who get involved are forced to engage with difficult and challenging issues to do with living the Christian life and being part of a church in cultural, political, social and interfaith contexts which are very different from our own.'

Basingstoke Community Churches

GLOBAL LINKS: *Zimbabwe, Kenya, and many others*

CONGREGATION SIZE (2003): *about 1,400 adults and children in six linked churches*

DENOMINATION: *Independent, members of Salt and Light Ministries*

Basingstoke Community Churches (BCC) began life as Basingstoke Baptist Church, a small and at times difficult congregation, until in the late sixties it was pastored by Barney Coombs, a pioneer in charismatic renewal and apostolic ministry. In 1970 a visiting speaker to the church, Peter Lyne, was preaching about the church in Antioch (see Acts 11 – 13) when he suddenly paused and said: 'I believe this church is to become an Antioch church, sending to and receiving from other nations.' This fitted with the kind of people who were being drawn to the church at that time, and became a core value for the church, and for what eventually became the wider Salt and Light family of churches.

Salt and Light Ministries

Salt and Light Ministries is an international family of
churches and leaders who linked together under the
leadership of Barney Coombs from the late sixties
onwards. Each church is independent but they
cooperate closely and share the following key insights
and values

- The Body of Christ is essentially 'relational' in
  character and make up
- Everyone in the church has a role to play within the
  Body
- Belief in apostolic ministry (see Ephesians 4)
- Belief in the Holy Spirit's ministry in the life and
  worship of the believer and the church, and
- Personal pastoring as a key to care, accountability
  and discipleship. The concept of 'spiritual
  fatherhood' has an important role.

By 2003, BCC had grown to a group of six churches in and
around Basingstoke, with some 1,400 adults and children in
their congregations. Members of BCC are serving Christ in
many countries of the world, and other members, young
and old, regularly go out on teams to work in many nations,
often supporting members of their own church who are
working on a longer term basis. The scale of their activity,
and the degree of action and enthusiasm for worldwide
mission demonstrated by church members, is breathtaking.

Dave and Chris Richards

In the mid-1970s, Dave Richards and his wife Chris were
leaders of a house church in Witney, Oxfordshire which asked

Barney Coombs for help and support. The Richards' had started out as Methodists, but because of their experience of the baptism in the Holy Spirit and a new-found conviction of the importance of believers' baptism, they were asked to leave that denomination. Through the seventies they increasingly networked with likeminded churches. Everything that followed grew out of relationships.

From 1979 Dave began to be involved with BCC. In 1981 he was invited to join the leadership team there (at which point he and Chris moved to the area with their family) and in 1983 he became the senior pastor. By that time the church had grown considerably through a model of house groups and local congregations, each actively involved in their local communities. To maintain unity and a shared vision, monthly celebrations were held, with all the congregations together. Dave had already been identified by others as having apostolic gifting. In 1996 he ceased being senior pastor in order to focus more on overseas mission work, but he still leads the apostolic team based at BCC and is accountable to that team.

Apostolic ministry

In the Salt and Light movement, as with some other 'New Church' movements, apostles are facilitators who care for and assist the development of churches and equip the saints for the work of ministry. According to 2 Corinthians 12:12, they demonstrate patience and can move in signs and wonders. They are also mobile, able to travel from place to place as needed.

Apostolic gifting in an individual is recognised and affirmed by other Christians within a church or fellowship.

Overseas links built through relationships

BCC has been involved in India since the mid-1970s, but over the years since then, links of friendship and mission work have been established in a number of countries. Asked how such links begin, Dave says, 'Look for a man! Somehow you get connected with certain people, in a joining by the Spirit. When such a meeting happens you just know that a significant relationship will develop. There is a spiritual dimension from a Kingdom perspective to such relationships. They are first and foremost about being together, in each other's homes and amongst each other's families. Doing things together grows out of the close relationships that develop.'

He cites the example of one of the earliest such links, begun in 1984 in Zimbabwe. 'I was in Harare on a speaking tour and one morning after speaking at a meeting of church leaders, there was a knock on my host's door. The young Zimbabwean pastor standing there asked me "Will you pastor me?" His name was Ngwiza Mkandela, and in the previous two years he had approached a number of church leaders in Zimbabwe with the same question, but all had refused. At that time pastoring of younger pastors by older people was not encouraged in most church circles. I agreed to the request and a strong relationship grew up which spread to both groups of churches and has been greatly enriching for both sides.' Basing his teaching on the lives of Paul and Timothy, Dave gave training and guidance in leadership which he has also given to church leaders in many other countries.

Ngwiza is now an expert in African church planting and an international consultant. Over twenty-five teams have gone out to Zimbabwe to work with his group of churches, and Ngwiza is received as an apostle and brother when he visits the Basingstoke churches. A similar relationship was established with Pastor J.B. Masinde from Nairobi, Kenya. His church is 8,500-strong and he oversees about one hundred and thirty other churches!

From 1990 a similar link was established with a group of churches in Sweden, through an apparently chance contact made by a member of BCC at a business conference. There are now regular visits in both directions between the two groups of churches, and some families from the two countries take holidays together. Swedes have joined members from BCC on joint mission teams to Africa.

One Swedish church in the group is outward-focused to an amazing extent. Started by a young couple as a Mexican restaurant between two nightclubs in the city of Vastaras, it now has 120 members, nearly half of whom are employed full-time by the church in providing a wide range of projects and facilities to serve the local community. Funding for their community work is supplied largely by the local city council. The church building is multi-purpose, with part of it serving as a restaurant for much of the week. The church also funds mission work in Calcutta through running a travel agency and a motorbike franchise!

BCC also has links with churches in many other countries. Church planting is under way in Spain and France, and there are workers in Uganda helping plant schools, undertaking special needs education, and running farms to support an orphanage and hospital. Teams regularly go to India, France, Bosnia and elsewhere.

There is a two-way flow of people between the linked churches, although for economic reasons there are inevitably more going out from the UK than come back from Africa or other countries in the south. In early 2003 BCC started supporting two new black Zimbabwean congregations in London and Sheffield, and were about to assist in the planting of a Kenyan congregation in London.

Global mission at the heart of church life

Mission – whether to the local community or other nations – is central to the life of the Basingstoke churches. It features in the preaching, the praying, the giving, and in church members constantly travelling to different parts of the world. All the current pastors have been involved in mission outside the UK at some time, and all are required to make at least one visit to another country each year.

Members of the churches are encouraged not to go on holiday to Mediterranean resorts where they will 'get burnt on the outside', but instead to take their families to visit poor communities in Africa or Asia, where they can 'get burnt on the inside' by seeing God at work. Business people in the congregation are encouraged to think in terms of what they can do for local Christians or churches in the places that they visit on business trips. Almost everyone who has been a member of the churches for five years or more will have been on an overseas mission trip at least once. Every so often the leadership will do a review of mission interest in the church and arrange to meet with every member to ask them: 'Has God put a nation on your heart? And if so, what are you going to do about it?'

The churches encourage people to use their varied gifting to serve in mission, whether directly or indirectly. Dave and Chris were enabled to go together on mission trips abroad when their children were young because another couple willingly looked after the children while they were away.

By faith, the churches run their own Christian school in Basingstoke, which educates about one hundred and eighty-five children aged from six to sixteen. The children are taught about mission and encouraged to go, with teams of young people from the school regularly going on mission trips as part of their school life. On reaching eighteen many of them will take a year out to serve God overseas before going on to higher education or employment. One example is the group of ten teenagers from BCC who planned to go to Kenya in August 2003. Their leader was a 20-year-old who had already lived in Kenya for a year working with street children. While out there, they were to be under the authority of a Kenyan youth pastor and engaged on projects proposed by the Kenyan church. Undergraduate members of the church who go on language placements as part of their degree, are encouraged to see this as a mission opportunity rather than just a chance for a good time. When Dave and Chris's daughter Becki went to Troyes in France for nine months as a language assistant at a local Lycee, she started a tiny Alpha group which grew steadily. Several other French-speaking students have since been based there. By early 2003 around twenty-five people were in L'Oasis (as it is now called), which has become a church plant led by Bob and Muriel Whitchurch. Becki loved this period, making contact with many 'not-yet Christians' in the town, university and local bars. A lot of the groundwork was done through a group that she and two other students formed to minister through music in such places. Her local Basingstoke congregation supported her in prayer and finance.

Mission activity is not confined to the young, however. Older people also have vital roles to play and often go as team members or leaders to different parts of the world. One team of older people has been to Sweden several times and another to Spain, seeing their main ministry as being to pray for the churches they have visited. Everywhere they have been, growth has occurred in the local churches. BCC also recognises that older people can play a valuable role in pastoring young leaders in recently established churches in parts of Africa and elsewhere. Those who may not be able to travel can also do great things. Four retired church members raised £15,000 to enable a couple working in Mozambique to buy a four-wheel drive vehicle.

Dave is keen not to give the impression that life has been one long success story for BCC and its mission ventures. 'There have been disappointments, heartbreaks, family pressures, thefts, and an apparently disastrous joint venture with a Canadian church to the Inuit people in Northern Canada. In one year three of BCC's local leaders died, but it was interesting to see the international turn-out at two of those funerals. What is clear is that overall God has blessed and used us to an astonishing extent to establish "Kingdom links" with his people round the world.'

Working with mission agencies

Within BCC there is such a wealth of firsthand experience of living in the countries which teams visit, that the churches themselves are usually able to provide training and practical support to those who go. When teams go to a place where there is already a well-established church with which they have links, they normally work in cooperation with the partner church rather than pursuing their own agendas.

But BCC are ready to work with mission agencies when this seems desirable. If BCC members feel called to work in specific countries or specialist areas of mission, the church may encourage them to contact a suitable agency to explore the possibility of being sent out by them. BCC does however expect to play a part in identifying placements, and in supporting and pastoring their members who go with agencies. 'Good alliances have been formed with CMS, Emmanuel International, YWAM, Tearfund and other agencies, over the years,' says Dave.

Two-way benefits from the links

When asked to summarise what benefits flowed from BCC's church-to-church links with other countries, Dave says: 'The benefits are nearly all one-way – in favour of the UK churches. Yes, British Christians can offer maturity and experience in the faith to help Christians in new churches. But I see a different dimension of living by faith among African Christians who, for instance, leave us standing in church planting.

'In Zimbabwe in particular, I have seen many church leaders modelling creative approaches to generating finance for churches and mission that I have not seen in the UK. For example, Ngwiza was teaching church leaders how to start up businesses. One way was through micro-enterprise; another was by training in strategic thinking. Ngwiza encourages his people to develop their skills, take risks in God and try to bring the Kingdom of God into their daily workplaces. The church folk have a variety of enterprises including financial services, kitchen and bedroom furniture, printing, and orthodontics. One pastor at thirty-seven years old is also the CEO of the ten most known hotels in the country, including the world-famous Victoria Falls Hotel.

'As I look back I am so grateful to the Lord for all he has done and will continue to do amongst us and our friends. We were recently away on a conference at which around thirty nations were represented. Each member of our International Team of 15 had brought a Joshua with them. As we prayed, studied the word, discussed and "strategised" together – Zimbabweans, Kenyans, Ugandans, Kiwis, Canadians, Indians, Americans and Europeans – we marvelled at what God has accomplished in our small family of Salt and Light in these last 30 years. We see small shoots emerging from the mustard seed revelation we had so many years ago. Our prayer is that one day there will be a mustard tree of the

Kingdom that will be a resting place for the birds of the air –
just as Jesus intended!'

14

Henley Baptist Church
and the Equip Trust

GLOBAL LINKS: *Kazakhstan*

CONGREGATION SIZE (2003): *about 85*

DENOMINATION: *Baptist*

'We have opened our doors to the west and all we've received is your sewage.' These words from a headmistress in Kazakhstan to Frank Payne, minister of Henley Baptist Church, in 1992 helped galvanise him and his church into a commitment to help the people of one region of Kazakhstan with training, professional advice, education, business exchanges and aid of many kinds. The results have been extraordinary.

Although the Baptist church in Henley-on-Thames is in a very affluent area, in economic terms its members are a

---

[3] Much of the early history of the Equip Trust recounted here is based, with permission, on the account given in *Small Church, Big Vision* by Lynn Green and Chris Forster, published by Marshall Pickering in 1995.

cross-section of the local population, and are not all highly paid professionals. Despite being a relatively small church, it has a big vision for global mission.[3] In addition to being a member of the Baptist Union, Henley Baptist is also part of the Salt and Light network of charismatic churches.

Birth of the vision

In autumn 1991 at a seminar in the UK, Frank Payne met Misha Grigoriyan, a Baptist leader from the Central Asian Republic of Kazakhstan. Misha spent a week at Henley Baptist before returning to Kazakhstan, and was attracted and impressed by the style and quality of the leadership in the Henley church, where genuine, deep relationships were valued. He was also inspired by the church's commitment to outreach and by its freedom in worship.

Frank learnt much from Misha about the situation in Kazakhstan – a country that he previously knew very little about. Misha invited Frank to visit his church in the area of South-Western Kazakhstan called Shymkent, in the belief that it would help revitalise his church. Frank went in 1992 along with two members of his congregation, one of whom, an entrepreneurial businessman, was just in the process of becoming a Christian.

Kazakhstan

Kazakhstan is one of the largest republics of the former Soviet Union and the ninth largest country in the world. Its population is around seventeen million, and it is rich in oil and other natural resources. It is also, however, relatively underdeveloped. Following the collapse of communism, much of the population live in poverty and its economy and civil institutions are weak by western standards. The population contains several ethnic groups, and ethnic tensions are an ongoing concern. The Government has been pursuing a policy of market liberalisation and moderate secularism and is keen for western involvement in strengthening the economy and institutions.

The work of Henley Baptist and the Equip Trust has focused on the South Kazakhstan region and especially the regional capital, Shymkent, which has a population of around three-quarters of a million.

60 per cent of the Kazakhstani people are at least nominally Muslim and about 25 per cent are nominally Christian, with unaffiliated churches and the Orthodox Church being the two largest groupings. Moslem missionaries from other countries have been very active there since the fall of communism.

On arrival Frank and his companions travelled round the region of Shymkent. Through Misha he made contact with a number of Government officials and became aware of their specific hopes and concerns for the area. One particular man he met was to become a key contact, Kuanish Bultayev, who had recently set up an agency to promote equal development between the region's hundred ethnic groupings. Bultayev is now the region's senator in the Kazakhstani Government and remains an important contact and friend.

The regional minister for education asked Frank to recruit teachers to work in Kazakhstan and also asked if he could facilitate a visit by some Kazakh English teachers to the UK. When Frank and his companions returned to Henley, the whole church became infected by their enthusiasm to help. Over a period of time 75 per cent of the congregation have become actively involved in the link with Kazakhstan: looking after the visitors who come, either as hosts, guides or drivers, raising funds, creating publicity, and loading containers; some have visited.

Productive partnership

In 1993 Frank and his original two companions visited Shymkent again and found even greater opportunities opening up. The Kazakhstani authorities were keen to seek their help in business and education, and plans were drawn up for establishing an English Language and Business Centre. By this time Frank was keenly aware that his own congregation could not hope by itself to meet all the needs with which it was being presented. There was the potential to start scores of business initiatives and dozens of English teachers were being requested. He had already sought help through the Baptist Union and the Salt and Light movement. They offered some assistance, but were not at that stage able to provide the in-country help needed to develop the many opportunities.

On his return from the second trip Frank therefore sought a partner, a step that has been repeated many times since then. Some YWAM leaders joined him on a joint visit to Shymkent, after which YWAM agreed to partner with Henley Baptist Church in Kazakhstan. YWAM were able to provide a field director to be based in Shymkent in order to start the work. Later others from YWAM and the Salt and Light churches provided a team of people to establish an English Resource Centre offering English language training and other skills and also to start a school.

Setting up the Equip Trust

At this time it became necessary to set up the Equip Trust to provide a suitable organisational and legal framework in which the partnership between the church and YWAM in Kazakhstan could flourish, and to enable others to be drawn into partnership. The Equip Trust was and remains essentially a venture of Henley Baptist Church, but welcomes contributions from many other individuals, churches and other organisations. After several years of productive partnership, by the late 1990s YWAM felt called to focus on a different area of Kazakhstan. It is now no longer actively involved in the work of the Trust, although good links continue between the two organisations.

Equip Trust projects in Kazakhstan

The Trust's work grew steadily, and by the end of 2002 it had about thirty people working in and around Shymkent. The majority are Kazakhstani, with some key staff from the UK. The Trust's vision has continued to be larger than the resources available and there is always more to be done, but a huge amount has been achieved in ten years. Projects include

- An English Resource Centre in Shymkent, offering English teaching and conversation and a library of English books and magazines, as well as general information on the UK. The courses it offers are enormously popular, and over two thousand people have attended them. There are plans to open a café there, in order to encourage conversations and friendship between Centre users and the staff
- The Salem school, which offers a rounded academic education to 85 children, aged five to thirteen. It is a private fee-paying school, with bursaries available for families who cannot afford the fees. The school was started in response to a request made by three Kazakhstani

teachers during the first teachers' conference organised by the Equip Trust. One subject on the curriculum which is not found in other schools is 'moral values'

- An English/Kazakh bakery, with equipment supplied from the UK, was started as a humanitarian project when bread queues were common in the city. Still running successfully ten years later, much was learnt in setting the bakery up, and useful experience was gained in UK/Kazkhstani partnership
- Shipping of containers supplying clothing, medicines, books and other equipment for orphanages and schools
- A programme for testing deaf children using audiometers supplied by the Equip Trust
- Bringing businessmen, educationalists, and other British people with professional skills to Shymkent for conferences, training, and exchanges of ideas and experience
- An experimental project to grow soya, which was begun in 2002 in partnership with Operation Agri and Feed the Children. If successful, soy milk will be produced for orphanage children, with the surplus being sold to provide funds for the orphanage
- The wife of the current British field director in Shymkent started trying to help one young mother with a child which had special needs. After a short time this mushroomed and she found herself running a unit for many children with special needs. The key elements of this work are a morning mixed-ability play school, afternoon therapy and parent training sessions. A three-year training course for special needs teachers and another for physiotherapy assistant, is being established to facilitate long-term development of the work. Relationships with five other units are being developed to expand the benefits of the work

- In 2002 students from Shymkent were assisted in coming to the UK for a few weeks in the summer to do farm work. The money earned helped pay for the students' college fees the following year
- A partnership is being established with a wheelchair factory in neighbouring Kyrgystan with a view to setting up a factory in Shymkent to help meet the enormous need for wheelchairs in Kazakhstan. This is in direct response to a request by the Deputy Minister of Health, who estimates a need for up to thirty thousand wheelchairs.

Speaking of the staff working in Kazakhstan, Frank points out that 'the Trust and its staff work in Kazakhstan as professionals. They offer their services and aid to anyone who will benefit, regardless of their religious background. They have been welcomed on the basis that they will contribute to development and modernisation in the region and not as Christian missionaries, and they are careful to respect this status. However the integrity and compassion which mark their work inevitably have an impact and this provides opportunities for the staff to talk about their faith. Wherever possible local Christians have been involved in the establishment and running of the Trust's projects and the Trust's involvement in Shymkent has in itself been an encouragement to the Christians there.

'Despite all that has been achieved, there is so much more that could be done. I am saddened by the way in which Shymkent has changed in the ten years that I've been visiting. The people and their leaders were desperate for support from the west in the huge task of reconstructing a nation, developing a market economy, and filling the spiritual vacuum left by communism. All too often though, they have received only the worst features of western culture – consumerism, materialism, pornography and gambling – and the city now reflects these imports. Unscrupulous businessmen have been quick to visit and promote their unsavoury wares. But few western Christians have shown an active interest in enabling this country which has so much potential to share in the positive elements of western life, or to open the eyes of its people to the Christian faith.'

Poland too!

Henley Baptist's global mission activities are not confined to Kazakhstan. In the late nineties Frank befriended a young Christian leader in Poland, through whom he built relationships with other Polish church leaders and invited them to Salt and Light events in the UK. The Salt and Light family of churches had, for a number of years, held an annual family camp, Days of Destiny, at the Harrogate agricultural show ground. Following a prophetic challenge to respond to the needs in mainland Europe, it was decided in 2001 to transfer this camp in smaller units to mainland Europe. Poland was a natural choice, with Henley Baptist Church coordinating at the UK end and Frank's Polish friends coordinating the Polish involvement. More camps are planned providing wonderful opportunities for members of UK churches to combine holidays with discipleship and evangelism.

Impact of global involvement on Henley Baptist Church

The vision and sacrificial giving of the members of Henley Baptist has underpinned the work of the Equip Trust from its origins to the present day, although other churches and organisations have also made valuable contributions. Frank says 'in 1992 we had a very clear word from God that if we gave what we had, God would add to it. We adopted a strategy that put overseas mission at the top of our list of priorities, then the local community and finally the local church. Our giving as a church community has reflected these priorities and amazingly over half a million pounds has been raised since 1992, largely by members and friends of Henley.' The church also released Frank, as senior pastor, to spend a considerable part of his time on building up the projects in Kazakhstan.

A good proportion of church members have actively supported the work in Kazakhstan, whether by going there to help, welcoming Kazakhstani visitors into their homes, giving towards the work or praying for it. They have had their hearts touched and their horizons widened by contact with people from such a different culture, and have truly given till it hurt. The 20 Kazakhstani students who came to the UK in summer 2002 to work on farms spent ten days at the end of their visit staying with church families and being given a cultural tour of the UK organised by church members. This is only one example of the open hospitality which has often been shown by the church. Another occurred during a visit by a team from Kazakhstan, when the church had the rich experience of a service conducted in Russian and English, in which one Russian-speaking lady was baptised and then renewed her wedding vows in a Christian context. Prayer meetings are always alive with the latest email news as the church begins to feel it has a commission to go into all the world.

It is astonishing that so much has been achieved by a church whose membership never exceeded 100 in those ten years. But it has not been without cost. Hardly any of the Trust's projects generate any significant income within Kazakhstan, so they continue to rely heavily on funding from the UK. The church has given willingly and from the heart, but has begun to feel drained by the financial burden. They continue to look for partners who will share the vision of the Equip Trust and be ready to contribute actively to its work. In addition to their global mission activities, the church is also actively involved in the local community, with a focus on supporting young people and their families. Their own church premises need modernisation and development to strengthen their local outreach. Over the next few years they may face some tough decisions.

'At times I wonder if the church is in danger of over-extending itself,' says Frank. 'This brings a tension between responding to the prophetic word which encouraged the church to give out in mission, and the wise counsel to build church in such a way that people are not burnt out and practical care is not missed. These are not easy issues and we continue to grapple with priorities and where the focus of our attention should be.'

Reflection

As Frank reflects on the last ten years, he says 'just as in Jeremiah's day – according to the message given him at the potter's house – the vessel of Israel needed reshaping, so the church in Britain today needs similarly to be reshaped. We are in a new world. A local church in its old traditional shape, meetings-based and sometimes reaching out will no longer connect to society. We must change the shape of the church; we must find new ways of expressing church and connecting to the world in which we live. Globalisation with the amazing development of English as the business language of the world means the local church can respond as never before to the Great Commission. Many have skills that are highly sought after in formerly closed countries like Kazakhstan. If ever there was a call to "come over and help us" it is now. In our local areas, the social needs and the positive attitude of the British Government to faith communities offer the same opportunity. The church must yield to the hands of the potter as he reshapes us to be far more flexible and involved in the world he loves.'

Frank Payne and the Equip Trust can be contacted at:

DaySpring Centre
55 Market Place
Henley on Thames
Oxon
RG9 2AA
Tel: 01491 577414
Fax: 01491 410775
Email: frank@equip.org.uk
Website: www.equip.org.uk

Afterword

It is our hope that these stories will prove to be an inspiration to many who are looking for something new. There are many lessons embedded in them and reading them is the best way to pick up some of the pearls of wisdom from those who have gone before. However, we also saw value in drawing out some of the common themes from the stories and presenting these as a summary of the message of this book.

1. Relationships are key

The common thread running through every single one of the stories in this book is that relationships are vital – in fact they are the key to making links with people in other parts of the world work. Relationships between the leaders of churches. Relationships with individuals who are being supported. Relationships with trusted intermediaries. It is these relationships that are the lifeblood, the bedrock for people and churches to work well together.

Some of these stories show how the development of communication links – even with many remote areas of developing countries – has done much to facilitate a growing sense of relationship and connectedness. Despite this however, it is clear that emails and phone calls are no substitute for meeting face to face. For people from very different cultures with very different ways of expressing themselves, being able to talk together, to live in each other's homes, share meals, pray together and worship together are essential parts of developing real relationships. Trust arises, differences can be communicated and explored, perceptions understood and faith in the same Lord become the shared experience that is the glue through thick and thin.

2. Size is not an issue

Many smaller churches in the UK might feel that their size prohibits them from having any meaningful interaction with the church globally. Their resources are more limited; they have fewer people to get involved in all the different areas of ministry that a larger church might have. Frank Payne from Henley Baptist would want to take issue with that argument! The work that has grown up out of a church of less than one hundred people is truly awe-inspiring. And Glebe Farm Baptist, a church of only twenty or so adults, really blows away the myth of size! There are ways that churches of every size can take on a global dimension, contributing to and learning from the global church.

3. Not just for the anoraks

When a church and its leadership have truly grasped a global vision, global mission can become something that the whole church gets involved with. The story of Basingstoke Community Churches bears witness to this truth. Over 50 per cent of the church family has visited one or more of their international links – that's more than seven hundred people! In so many churches one hears the lament from the Mission Committee that they can't get the young people interested. Yet our young people are the global generation! They are growing up in a world which is becoming ever more interconnected. Maybe the old ways of doing the mission slot in the service or praying for 'our missionaries' are simply not firing their imagination. Maybe what they need is to go and see for themselves; to lend a hand building a clinic or painting an orphanage, running a youth camp or getting to know other young people in another part of the world. Many of the stories in this book show how churches have got their whole congregation (young people included) involved in global mission – where will you start?

4. Keeping it in the family

There are a number of examples in this book of churches that have built successful partnerships with churches of the same denomination. But before leaping to any conclusions it is also important to recognise the success and effectiveness of other examples in which churches have created a partnership with a church of a different denomination. The message seems to be – follow whatever path seems to work for you. There are ways of making partnerships work both within and across denominations.

5. You'll never be the same again

In most of the stories we've quoted some of the things that people from the churches have said about their experience of global mission. Part of the reason for this is that so many of these people have been dramatically changed by their experience of the global church. Families from Birmingham who have had Brazilians staying in their homes, people from Manchester who have visited Uganda and come back transformed by the experience. Stepping out of our comfort zones and the confines of our own situation and culture can be a daunting experience but can also open us up to allow God to change and shape us in ways that would be impossible if we simply stuck with what we know.

But the positive impact is not just on individuals. Almost all of the case studies in this book demonstrate how whole churches can be transformed through interaction with the global church. Do you want to see your church being transformed, with people more committed, more involved, more intimate with God? The stories in this book suggest that one route to achieving this that God seems to bless, is involvement in global mission. The church in the west has so much to learn from our Christian brothers and sisters in other parts of the world.

6. Mission at the heart of church life

Much is being made of the transition from modernity to post-modernity[4] with much discussion in the Christian world about what churches should look like and be in the coming decades. The transition appears to be from a focus on 'doing church' (churches pouring their energies into their internal life and activities) to a focus on 'being missional' (churches recognising mission as the role of the community of believers). As we said in the Introduction: mission, whether round the corner or halfway across the world, should be the heartbeat of the church. We hope that the stories in this book show that it is possible – even desirable – for global mission to be central to church life and not peripheral to it.

7. Global inspiring local

Some of the stories show what an impact a church's global involvement can have on its local community. Altrincham Baptist through their link in Uganda has brokered the

---

[4] For more background to this discussion see the first book in this series: *Connect!* by Tim Jeffery with Steve Chalke.

twinning of their town with that Ugandan city. Visits by local dignitaries and politicians have led to a partnership that has gone well beyond the church, opening up many different avenues of cooperation and understanding. A good example of salt being salty perhaps?

For many people, involvement in global mission has radically changed their outlook on local mission. People who have experienced church life and work in a different part of the world tend to think differently about the role of their own church within its local community. It appears that it can sometimes be easier to get involved outside of one's own local context and then bring back a new enthusiasm and understanding.

8. Dealing with setbacks

It would be wrong to paint a simplistic, purely rosy picture of global church partnerships. The stories in this book have not been chosen and edited to be some glossy advert for how easy it all is. They include the difficulties and heartache, the painful decisions and mistakes that are inevitably a part of any partnership. What is so impressive about so many of the stories here is the way that people have handled, learnt and moved on from the setbacks that they have encountered. The commitment and relationships that have developed seem to have helped them weather the storms and not simply give up when the going has got tough.

We hope that you have been challenged and inspired by these stories. If you do want to explore further how your church could get involved in this new era of global mission, make contact with Connect! at www.connect.nu or directly with one of the Connect! partners whose details are given on the following pages.

Notes on the agencies behind the Connect! Initiative

About Connect

Connect is an initiative that is seeking to help the Christian community in the UK grapple with and make the most of the massive changes happening in global mission.

Connect recognises that
- Globalisation, post-modernity and changes in the global church have fundamentally changed the context for mission
- Local churches are becoming a key player in global mission
- The future of global mission will be characterised by a growing diversity in how mission is done and by whom.

Connect has been established to help foster this new era in mission, encouraging churches to get involved in global mission in appropriate ways and working in the more established mission community to help them respond positively to these changes.

A group of agencies has come together in partnership to seek together to be 'cheerleaders' for this new era in global mission under the banner of Connect.

For more information on Connect, please visit the website
www.connect.nu
or call us on 020 7450 9000

1. About All Nations Christian College

Our Mission Statement

The purpose of All Nations Christian College is to
train and equip men and women for effective
participation in God's mission in our multi-cultural
world.

Located just to the north of London in the beautiful setting
of Easneye Estate in the Hertfordshire countryside, All
Nations has been one of Europe's leading centres for the
training of cross-cultural mission workers for over three
decades. As well as the popular Certificate, Diploma and
BA or MA Degree courses in mission studies, All Nations
is now offering a unique Sports Leadership and
Intercultural Studies module in partnership with
Christians in Sport and from September 2003, a Certificate
level course in the Arts and Intercultural Studies.

All Nations staff include thirteen academic tutors with a
wealth of mission understanding and cross-cultural
experience. The 150 or so students also come from every
corner of the world. Most have already had some cross-
cultural experience. Some have been mission workers for
several years. Most have a professional qualification; many
are graduates. Some are mothers with young children;
some will have babies while they are at college! This
exciting mix of ages and ethnic backgrounds, ability and
experience makes All Nations what it is best at . . .
preparing you to live and work anywhere in God's world.

Flexibility and choice are important to our students. We
have always tried to have a tailor-made course suitable for
each individual need. It is not necessary to be an academic

'high flyer' to study at All Nations Christian College.

On the other hand, if you are looking for something that will stretch you intellectually, there is plenty here for you too. The college is approved by the Open University Validation Service and offers Open University validated awards.

For more information see our website
www.allnations.ac.uk
   or email info@allnations.ac.uk

2. CMS (Church Missionary Society)

CMS is a movement of people in mission, obeying the call of God to proclaim the Gospel in all lands and to gather people into the fellowship of Christ.

Having grown out of the anti-slavery movement, CMS was founded in 1799 and works with partners in over 50 countries, including Britain, where more than 4,000 local churches support its work.

Our mission is to go "where Jesus' name is rarely heard"

· on the margins
· among young people and children
· in the cities
· among many faiths
· in a materialistic world

www.cms-uk.org
Church Mission Society, Partnership House,
157 Waterloo Road, London SE1 8UU
Tel. 020 7928 8681 Fax. 020 7401 3215
Registered Charity No. 220297

Church Mission Society

3. Global Connections

In a world where there can either be so much choice it overwhelms you or so few alternatives to suit you, Global Options helps churches find the right options for them.

From churches who are trying a completely fresh approach to mission to those needing a specialised piece of information, Global Options is there to help.

As a network of organisations, churches and individuals committed to world mission Global Connections is in a unique position with a bird's eye view of world mission. We can find all the good resources from the network, call on the experts, and learn from leaders so that even if we don't know the answer we know a man who does!

Is your church making world choices?

Tel: 0870 774 3806
Email: options@globalconnections.co.uk
Web: www.globalconnections.co.uk

4. Oasis Trust

   Helping you to *Go Global*

Oasis is the founding partner of the Connect! initiative and is committed to the development of global mission into and out of the UK. Working alongside local churches, Oasis is active in 15 countries of the world. We seek to be a channel through which individuals and churches can get involved in practical action with groups of poor and marginalised people and with other Christians across the world.

> The **Oasis Global Opportunities** programme offers a range of options in 15 countries. Placements in teams are available from 2 weeks to 10 months. Individual placements for people with professional skills are available from just a few weeks to many years. Opportunities also exist for tailor-made visits by church groups.

If your church is looking for a project to take on, a church to partner with or you simply want to discuss the options open to you, we would love to hear from you.

For further information please contact us:
Website: www.oasistrust.org
Email: globalaction@oasistrust.org
Tel: 020 7450 9000

5. Radstock Ministries

Radstock's vision for mission starts with a truth about God – he is a missionary God. Ever since he went looking for Adam and Eve in the Garden, God has been seeking and saving lost people. That missionary nature is most clearly and unambiguously revealed by the cross. Christ crucified defines God as a missionary God. But Christ crucified also highlights a second truth – about the church. God's church is a missional church. Our message, our ministry, our lifestyle are all shaped by the cross. We are those who have taken up their cross. A third truth about mission rounds out our vision: mission reflects the character of the God who initiates it. So mission is relational. Mission is compassionate. Mission is sacrificial.

Radstock's goal is to see local churches taking up the biblical privilege and responsibility of mission. They have church-based mission practitioners available to come alongside your church leadership to offer analysis, consultation and assistance as you develop a whole-church commitment to local and global mission. They are committed to long-term, low-key, relational ministry. Their approach is guided by principle while being adapted to the challenges of global mission today.

If you want to explore getting your church connected for mission in Russia, Ukraine, the Baltics, the Balkans, Central Asia, China or Southern Africa through Radstock Ministries, their contact details are

Radstock Ministries
2a Argyle Street
Mexborough
South Yorkshire
S64 9BW

Tel: 01709 582345
Website: www.radstock.org
Email: info@radstock.org